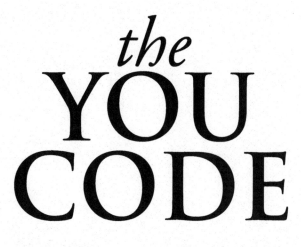

the
YOU
CODE

YOUR NEW LIFE MAP HIDDEN
IN YOUR ANCIENT GENES

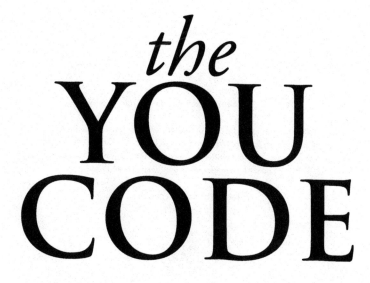

the YOU CODE

YOUR NEW LIFE MAP HIDDEN IN YOUR ANCIENT GENES

JAMES SHERIDAN

DUDLEY COURT PRESS
SONOITA, AZ

Published by Dudley Court Press
www.DudleyCourtPress.com

Publisher's Cataloging-in-Publication Data
Names: Sheridan, James, 1970- author.
Title: The YOU code : your new life map hidden in your ancient genes / James Sheridan.
Description: Sonoita, AZ : Dudley Court Press, [2020]
Identifiers:
ISBN: 978-1-940013-76-3 (paper)
978-1-940013-81-7 (ebook)
LCCN: 2020914669
Subjects:
LCSH: Self-help techniques. | Self-actualization (Psychology) | Self-realization.
Human behavior—Genetic aspects. | Personality—Genetic aspects.
Human genetics. | Nature and nurture. | Medical genetics. | Genetic genealogy.
Genotype-environment interaction. | Interpersonal relations.
Interpersonal communication. | Success.
BISAC: BODY, MIND & SPIRIT / New Thought.
SELF-HELP / Personal Growth / General.
SELF-HELP / Motivational & Inspirational.
Classification:
LCC: BF632 .S447 2020
DDC: 158.1—dc23

Cover and interior design by Dunn+Associates, www.Dunn-Design.com

More from James Sheridan at www.JamesSheridan.com
Read James Sheridan's daily thoughts on Twitter @FlySheridan

For you, both of you.

"If the doors of perception were cleansed every thing would appear to man as it is: Infinite. For man has closed himself up, till he sees all things thro' narrow chinks of his cavern."

—WILLIAM BLAKE

Contents

Your great journey inward begins at the beginning of time. Solve
the mystery of where your inherent nature comes from and why
it's the key to your new life map.

Reveal what you once were and what's still living inside you as you
identify your inherited, genetic personality template (Genetype),
and cut away your nurture from your nature. This is a search and
rescue mission for your soul.

Success is subjective. Based on your newly discovered Genetype,
discover why you're here and what your purpose is. Uncover the
job description written into your ancient genes that defines you
and grants you passage to the Bliss State.

Love and relationships. Discover how knowing Genetypes leads
to harmonious relationships, and the crucial balance that played a
pivotal role in our distant past.

Special thanks to the thousands of people across the world who became my research subjects and beta testers over the last decade for the core theory of this work; from the focus groups, the seminar attendees, the clients, and the friends, to the unsuspecting strangers on barstools, the expressions on your faces empowered my every word. Thank you to the people who helped me bring this to life: Gail Woodard and the Dudley Court Press team (Carrie, Celia, Lora, Teresa, and Wilma), Kathi Dunn, Tina Nguyen, and Emily Heckman. Thanks, Jack Canfield, for your validation and support. And thank you to my old history teacher, Mr. Bearman, for only encouraging my endless questions.

part one

THE
QUEST

Leopards, Scorpions, and You

There is an old saying: *Leopards can't change their spots.* In other words, it's in our nature to act a certain way, and our basic personality never changes. This isn't cynical; it's powerful. Why should leopards change their spots, their edge, the camouflage that lets them realize their purpose to be hunters? If a leopard were to hunt out of its natural environment, in a gray urban area, would it lose its edge of camouflage and quickly be spotted by its prey? If a leopard were captured and caged, or forced to carry hay around a farm, would the leopard's spirit fade away? Like the leopard, we too are animals, but we are disconnected from, and hidden from, our true nature. My mission is to help you find your "spots" and show you how to best use them in this contemporary jungle, to acquire tailor-made happiness and prosperity.

The leopard's life map is in its ancient genes, a biological blueprint that defines its natural behavior patterns. Each leopard will have a different *nurture* experience since birth, *but they are still leopards.* Humans are much more complex animals with more complex needs and desires, but we also have a biological blueprint that defines our natural behavior patterns, and ours varies between members of the same species. My focus is on you uncovering and reconnecting to your *biological* nature, and disconnecting from your *biographical* nurture.

Of course, nurture does affect our behavior and can cause desirable outcomes, but it's not the path to our true self and finding our purpose. Humans are inclined to polarize opinions, so we take extreme sides on the "nature *versus* nurture" argument, but the reality is that both our nature *and* our nurture unconsciously affect our behavior. With awareness and perhaps professional help we can identify and overcome the nurtured behaviors that can be so self-sabotaging, and this is the side of us that we can and should change. But trying to change the nature we're born with is like trying to separate our shadow; *it's who we are.* Once you know who and what you are, everything in life suddenly falls into place because your inherent purpose becomes obvious, and this plots a course to happiness on a life map that's specific to you.

Life is a journey down a corridor of dilemmas, always a door to choose. Should I marry this person or not? Should I take that job or not? Should I move home? We choose a door, and then a whole new corridor of dilemmas opens up as we continue this journey, an endless web of binary choices and outcomes. Without having the right life map, our decision making is haphazard, wrong, or simply nonexistent. What skews our judgment in that corridor are the voices of our past: parents, teachers, society, all the people who've scratched away at our true self. But the voice most worth listening to is the one that resonates with your *nature*. What often stops us listening to this voice of our nature is that it seems to originate from a place buried deep inside us, *almost with a life of its own*, so we have trouble trusting it. This voice is a collect call from your ancient genes, sometimes called a "gut instinct." Some gut instincts are common to all humans, and some are specific to certain groups of humans. Some gut instincts should be listened to, some should not, and some should be adapted to modern life. So, making good choices is also about which door *not* to choose, as a well-known parable illustrates:

A scorpion asked a frog a question: "I want to get across the river. If I sit on your back, will you swim me across?" The frog replied, "No! If I do that, you'll sting me to death." The scorpion said, "Why would I do that? If I did, you'd sink, and we would both drown." The frog accepted the scorpion's explanation and agreed to the request. Halfway across the river, the scorpion stung the frog. Sinking, the frog said, "Why did you do that? Now we will both die!" The scorpion said, "I'm sorry. It's just my nature." Both the scorpion and the frog drowned.

I don't condemn the scorpion for stinging the frog; I condemn it for not respecting its inherent nature and making a bad choice as a result. A scorpion should not be taking rides on other animals to get across the river; it simply needs to stay on this side of the river or find another way to cross. That's not defeatist; it's efficient. It's the natural line of least resistance across its life map. Whenever we have to hack a path through The Universe with brute force, it usually means we are on the wrong path. Not that the goal can't be achieved, but it might not ultimately make us happy.

The frog knew of the scorpion's nature, but it didn't act upon the knowledge, so the frog is as much to blame. Here you will learn not only what your own nature is, but also that of *others*, practically to the point of reading their minds and anticipating their actions and reactions. And you will stop wishing other people could change and be more like you, because you will then know their inherent and immovable nature. Understanding others leads to acceptance of others, and acceptance leads to inner peace. Reality, not fantasy, is the bridge to an authentic life experience.

Recovering and embracing your inherent nature is not only the line of least resistance, it's the key to revealing who and what you are and precisely what your purpose is. When you've identified *and accepted* your true nature, something magical happens in that corridor of life choices: the correct door for you pings open automatically, and you confidently walk through it, into a new corridor, where the next door does the same. I will help you define what type of "gut" you have and to interpret exactly what it's saying so you're more confident about listening to it, and so its voice stops getting muffled by nurtured forces and the cookie-cutter life map society wants you to use.

Success is Subjective

Where should a life map take us? Modern society gives us a moral compass at birth, with parents, teachers, politicians, and corporations nurturing the way to a vague and generic goal we call "success," dubiously defined as the attainment of prosperity. The implication is that we all want the same thing and it's measured in residential square footage and digits on a bank balance. But how can this be true when we see so many "successful" people having the same problems as those considered not as successful? A-list movie stars in rehab are an example of this.

I've personally witnessed multimillionaires having nervous breakdowns, addicted to antidepressants, and in some cases I've seen their destruction. I have built and sold million-dollar companies, lived in million-dollar homes, and at one point in my life I simultaneously owned an Aston Martin car, an airplane, and a thirty-five-foot yacht. At that time I experienced deep unhappiness, not necessarily *because* I was so "successful," but rather because, from a personal happiness point of view, I was no better off than when I was not successful. Conversely, I've shaken hands with people literally living in gutters in Thailand who appeared to be the most intrinsically happy people I've ever met. Something is wrong with this picture when framed by the common idea that we all must shoot for this generic goal of "success," and recent surveys perhaps explain why: the level of personal satisfaction increases proportionately with annual income only up to $50–70,000 and then plateaus.

Happiness is our common goal, not success. Success is incorrectly perceived as a means to that end (for most people, anyway, as you shall see). A person who sets any goal, success included, surely assumes that the end result is happiness, or what would be the point of the goal? But even if we are able to rebel against our nurtured programming of striving for success and to strive for happiness instead, we aren't much better off because it leaves us with the perpetually elusive task of finding happiness, defined as a sense of contentment with life. At least success is something one can begin to paint a bull's-eye on, so it's hardly surprising we default to this goal instead.

Modern medicine attempts to define happiness as something directly proportionate to serotonin levels in the brain, and so considers brain-chemistry-altering drugs, such as antidepressants, to be the solution. Putting the known side effects of drugs to one side, we all sense human happiness to be something more than a pill can provide. To simply cross out the "bitter" in "bittersweet" seems childish, even inhumane, and our gut knows it.

We spend vast mental resources asking what the meaning of life is, as if knowing the answer will make us happy, but the question is never answered. There is only meaning to *you* and your place in The Universe. If I were now able to prove to you that the meaning of life is an invisible cat that rests our planet on its head, what could you do with that information (apart from being kinder to cats)? What's the meaning of a flower? There is no meaning; it just is.

The only "meaning of life" that has any pointed utility is the kind that's specific to *you,* the kind I will lay out for you and that ultimately contributes to a universal meaning of life. We must stop looking for an external answer to all our problems and instead look in the mirror at what simply *is,* and let The Universe unfold according to its natural design and the life map it has uncannily built into each of us. *There* is where you will find this elusive "sense of contentment with life" defined as happiness, the ultimate goal of all humans.

To find The Answer, I had to ask the right question. After peaking early as an airline captain at twenty-nine years old, I started businesses, traded financial markets, and invested in real estate. I then passed on my experiences to others through the self-improvement industry, and that's where I've fought on the front lines for the past twenty years. So it's been most of my life's work to attempt to define happiness, because teaching something effectively forces one to bottle it into a formula anyone can access. It's been a challenge, and this book represents the hard-won solution.

It's one thing to teach the principles of happiness, but it's another to instill the practice. The student often unconsciously rejects an ideological implant because inception of the idea is not organically of the student's nature. A great deal of self-improvement material of every subgenre, be it success/happiness/diet/relationships/etc., requires the student *to change their nature,* effectively asking a leopard to change its spots. No wonder, then, why New Year's resolutions fade, gym memberships are forsaken, and self-improvement books are enjoyed but forgotten. It's an attempt to build skyscrapers on sand. This was a frustrating reality for me, someone who made it his goal in life to help people get what they want. I grew weary of taking horses to water, nay (pardon the pun), of grabbing the horse's mane and thrusting its snout into the water but not having it drink. *Clearly, the horse preferred a different beverage.* After this revelation, after *I* looked in the mirror, I found the answer, and it's changed *my* life forever, on all levels, including how I teach the subject of happiness. Now it will change yours.

Different beverages for different "horses" are the key. It's not about what society wants for you or what has been nurtured into you, *it's about what your specific nature already has mapped out for you, the life map you were clutching at the second of your conception.* No matter what your parents and teachers said you were and what you would or should become, your optimal path through life was *premade* by an indomitable force that, once recognized and energized, automatically and totally overrides nurturing. I'm not talking about some specific fortune-told event, I'm talking about a map, a means of navigation with a set range of options best suited to your needs.

Success is subjective, and its definition varies wildly from one individual to the next. The societal map is a round hole, and you are a peg that is one of several shapes, some of them round, but most are not. Generality has been the roadblock on our path to happiness. "Everyone benefits from meditation." *Some* people do. "Everyone wants to be rich and successful." *Some* people do. "Every man needs a career." *Some* men do. "Everyone needs to be beautiful." *Some* people do. "Every woman needs to be a wife/ mother." *Some* women do. "Every woman should have a career." *Some* women should. You get the point, but not nearly as much as you shall in Part Two. By the same principle, your opinion of what *other people's* life maps should be is as irrelevant, arrogant, and hopeless as society's because it's baked into other people's *nature.* You'll soon see how even political biases are influenced by our nature. (Why do you think it's always a 50/50 fight? Is something keeping us in balance?) This principle is *why* Dale Carnegie was so correct to say, "Nobody wins an argument," in *How to Win Friends and Influence People*. This is powerful in the peace it brings you because personal suffering partially ends when you stop arguing with other people's unchangeable nature, you stop giving piggyback rides to scorpions, and you instead celebrate our invisible diversity.

"Know thyself" is the most resonant, and ancient piece of advice ever given, the instruction is practically welded into our genes, beckoning us to each heroically embark on the ultimate and inevitable journey within. Don't *change* who you are; *awaken* to it. You can accomplish anything, but there's only one thing you should, and I will explain how this one thing is encoded into your nature. So, the next question is: How can you "know thyself"? What is your true nature?

Biological Blueprints

To appreciate how your specific life map could possibly be hidden in your ancient genes, let's first understand where your genes have come from and why, and how much they mean to you as an individual. As a backdrop to open your mind, consider the two crucial questions that remain unanswered by science: Where did the first organism on earth come from? Where can consciousness be found in the human anatomy? Perhaps we will never know, and perhaps we aren't meant to know. The point is that even modern science isn't omniscient.

In the absence of scientific answers for everything, there is room for theory and what I refer to as "common sense science," a theory based on a substantial body of evidence, anecdotal or not, that makes sense to us beyond a reasonable doubt and has a big-picture advantage over conventional science, which is bound by the exclusive use of logic. The *sole* use of logic to explain *emotional* beings is an oxymoron child of patriarchal thinking, and it's better to use our entire brain than only one (logical) half of it. Half-brained dogma is also indicative of how unbalanced humanity has become, something I will discuss more as the book unfolds. We could spend a lifetime searching for "smoking-gun" proof for everything, but it would be a lifetime wasted if deprived of happiness in the meantime. But let's start with what we know.

For over four billion years, an energy field of debated origin has vigorously fought for life to survive and thrive on this otherwise ordinary rock we call earth, using a brilliantly intricate biological blueprint. This process occurred at a glacial pace, with The Energy Field having a primary goal of organisms reproducing. Each generation of reproduction gives The Energy Field the opportunity to select the choicest features from each of the mating organism's biological blueprint to create superior offspring, thus constantly improving and adapting each species for best chance of survival. These biological blueprints of self-replicating (hence *energy*-related) material are referred to as DNA (deoxyribonucleic acid), and the components of it are referred to as "genes." Each generational evolution is a mutation of those parental genes, so we are all mutants. Because this process of genetic mutation is so ancient, science has learned much about where we came from as a species and as individuals of that species.

This grinding process of genetic mutation occasionally causes dramatic changes to the biology of a species, the goal always being to make it more able to survive in its environment. An example of this is the earliest humans standing on their hind legs for the first time, freeing up their front legs to evolve into arms to make tools, throw spears, and create fire. Then, becoming hunters, our fur was shed in favor of sweat glands, an ingenious cooling mechanism that allowed us to run for longer distances (not speeds) than the animals we hunted, suddenly catapulting humans to the top of the food chain.

The Energy Field doesn't appear to discriminate between species of organism or have any favorites; it simply wants the strongest life form to prevail. Consider that a single microorganism could win a decisive genetic war against humans; it simply wants to survive the same as us, and The Energy Field has evidently provided it with the weapons to do so, as The Black Death demonstrated by wiping out a third of all humans in medieval Europe. Almost 10% of human DNA is made of viruses, our ancient battle scars from this ongoing genetic war.

In short, any nature embedded in your ancient genes would have been hard-pressed to survive to the present day, so it presumably would've had a purpose for our survival as a species. So, is your nature in your genes? If so, how far back does this genetic link go?

In Your Nature

For proof of human nature being both genetic *and ancient*, you only have to know what's behind our common modern-day behaviors. Why, when dinner guests arrive, despite the host sporting that "simply must have" living area and dining room, do the guests all congregate in the kitchen? Could granite countertops be our contemporary campfire, a genetically implanted memory of a long and ancient past when the campfire (ancient kitchen) was where we huddled together for warmth and safety? And when those guests become jealous of the "simply must have" living area and dining room of the host's house, why do they feel so compelled to keep up with The Joneses? Because we have an inherent need to conform, to fit in with the "tribe," because that meant survival. In ancient times you literally had to huddle and keep up (with The Joneses) or a predator might see you as easy prey and pick you off.

As these guests dine enthusiastically, we wonder: why do we compulsively devour a burger or a tub of ice cream so fast? This "gorging gene" is human nature inherited from our past; if an ancient human saw a tree heaving with ripe fruit, without refrigeration facilities the only sensible thing to do was to eat as much of it as possible and as quickly as possible before some other animal came along to feast on the human as well as the fruit (thanks to insulin, our bodies storing the surplus calories as fat to get us through harder times). Our ancient senses in the present day act the same way when we encounter fatty or sweet foods high in calories, which is great for energy storage in ancient times but catastrophic in modern, which is why health must be a feature of our life map that we address later in the book. "Limited time offer!" advertising slogans and investment manias work so well on us also possibly because of the gorging gene, something we'll also come back to later on because any life map also has to deal with financial matters.

Over coffee and dessert at this soiree, a conversation about adolescent daughters and dress code comes up, everyone shaking their heads over why their children appear to be growing up faster and why puberty is getting younger. This is happening because, in our current times of relative prosperity, nature is telling females that now is a good time to have offspring, while the going is good so you can feed them. The so-called "Hemline Index" even became an economic theory in 1926: the principle that hemlines on skirts and dresses rise in line with stock prices. The Energy Field cares about reproduction, not our contemporary taboos or the social narrative *du jour*.

For some after-dinner fun, the hostess teaches her guests line dancing. As they finally all move to the beat in perfect synchronicity with one another, loins stir and an inexplicable sensation of unity sweeps over them, almost like a trance. This is likely a legacy of our tribal dances, often during festivals and revered rites-of-passage ceremonies that sometimes lasted days, a deeply spiritual event, not a frivolous one.

Eventually the guests go home and the exhausted hosts collapse in bed and fall asleep so fast that one of them almost rolls off the bed, but they awaken in time to stop the fall. Why do we automatically awaken from even the deepest sleep to catch our fall when we roll off the edge of a bed? This is a genetically inherited instinct from when we slept in trees millions of years ago.

Next morning, as these hungover hosts clear up, they receive texts of touching gratitude from their guests, and they feel a wave of joy sweep over them. Why should acts of kindness make us feel good and acts of meanness make us feel bad? Is there something in our ancient genes to explain this? I shall offer an explanation at the conclusion of the book.

Let's look at some more abstract and anecdotal evidence of a "nature gene" inherited from our ancient past. Sensual experiences can be like keys that unlock unconscious memories that are not our own. You've probably experienced *déjà-vu*, a sense of previously experiencing a place or situation before, despite knowing that there was no possible way that could be so. How can we explain that? Hindus (one of the oldest religions) would argue that it is memories of your past life and that your soul is stuck in an eternal loop of birth, death, and rebirth until you finally live the right life by correcting all your wrongdoings. If you were to challenge them by proclaiming that you don't remember your death, they would reply: "Do you remember your *birth*?" "I must have done something wrong in my past life," we say without thinking. Explain a true love between twin souls, when two lovers feel half of a whole, when their union feels more like *re*union, after being together for what seems like centuries before. Romantic relationships are a crucial part of any life map, so we will address the subject of love later on, once your true nature has been recovered and dusted off, because only then can it be successfully paired with another's.

Can our dreams provide evidence of our nature not only being inherited and ancient, but also containing memories of distant ancestors? The more abstract dreams sometimes require translating from ancient meaning. A common dream is for males to be bitten in the genitals by a snake. Certain ancient rites-of-passage rituals may explain this: as young teens were separated from their mothers to be circumcised, they were told that their foreskins were made as an offering to a serpent god (serpents a constant feature in human mythology and theology, the shedding of skin symbolic of rebirth). A common dream for romantically dissatisfied females is to be followed by a male who has an animal's head, such as those on pagan gods, most notably in Egyptian mythology. This has been linked to an unconscious yearning for a more spiritual connection with, and *equality* with, a romantic partner, the type of relationship that existed more in our ancient matriarchal past. As Nietzsche said, "In our sleep and dreams we pass through the whole thought of earlier humanity."

Today, society tends to see ancient polytheist "heathens" as idiots, but from a genetic perspective, 2,000 years of monotheist conditioning is no match for *at least* 68,000 years of polytheist living (a single god getting 2.8% of our genetic memory imprints versus multiple gods getting 97.2%). Whatever your current faith, and not to disrespect or discount it, it's hardly surprising we each harbor such memories within us, however much we try to repress or disapprove of them.

So, the nature of our *species* is both inherited and ancient, but is our *individual* nature inherited? As I write in 2020, proof of individual nature being inherited comes from the rapidly changing frontiers of genetic science. A monogamy gene has been discovered in male mice, the left-handed gene has been discovered in humans, and more evidence is emerging.

If individual nature is inherited, where does it come from? The obvious and perhaps popular answer would be parents. But if that's completely true, how do we explain the common phenomenon of multiple children with the same parents and same upbringing and even same sex being so different from one another and, most of all, having inherently different natures from their parents? "I don't know where she gets it from," say the parents, scratching their heads, wondering if she's "the black sheep."

We often observe offspring exhibiting idiosyncrasies of their parents, but we must not confuse the mimicking aspect of nurture with the realities of genetic nature. We may also observe some inconsequential and isolated physical or mental quirks in offspring that seem so unique that they could have only possibly come from the parents' genes, but my focus is on the utilitarian side of our nature, specifically in preset and hardwired personality *frameworks*— something I will explain shortly.

A common cause of family strife is parents' and their offspring's basic personalities being about as compatible as oil and water, and this is because *a genetically inherited personality framework isn't from parents*; it just hops around generation after generation at random. I've learned this firsthand in my research, and it stands to reason when applying what we now know about how genetics work. Consider how it's biologically possible for white-skinned parents to have a brown-skinned baby and vice versa, evidently *because genes can belong to a past far more distant than parents*. You will see more truth in this as the book unfolds.

To recap, our "nature" is the true *biological* self (made of genes), whereas our "nurture" is the false *biographical* self (made of ego) that society has imposed on our true self. We each seek a map to ultimately acquire happiness, but the definition of happiness will vary from one person to another because we don't all share the same biological blueprint. These biological blueprints have skipped around the gene pool for millions of years, and our nature is not necessarily inherited from our parents.

If we decode your true nature from your ancient genes, you will be able to define what happiness means to you, which means you will have a new defined life-goal, and you will know the best path to take on the map of life. Our final question, then, is: how do we find an individual's specific nature? That is the question I have dedicated the last decade of my life to answering.

Riddles Are the Answer

Our first step to excavating your true nature is to know where to dig. Is our individual nature only a smorgasbord of infinite combinations that have no meaning, or do common and set *patterns* exist, narrowing down our excavation area? Thankfully for our search, each of us isn't as "special" as we might think. Humans have a great deal more in common with each other than we believe, at least when it comes to what I call "genetic disposition frameworks."

A genetic disposition framework is a *cloned template* of ingrained and interrelated traits that stem from a single dominant and defining driver of its host. It is more than a personality type; personality types are the hybrid of nature and nurture and can have limited application and a compromised fit to the individual.

———

A Genetype is a *cloned template* of ingrained and interrelated traits that stem from a single dominant and defining driver of its host.

———

For the sake of brevity and brain fry, I will abbreviate "genetic disposition framework" to genetic type, or "*Genetype*" (pronounced "jenna-type"). The good news for your quest to "know thyself" is that there are only fourteen Genetypes to choose from, further narrowing down to only seven for each sex, as you will see in the next chapter. Remember, we are talking about your biological nature, not your biographical nurture; the hybrid of the two is what results in a perceived infinite number of "special" people, but *nature* is what we are concerned with. I'm soothing your panicked ego (that believes it's "special") for now, but we must soon push it aside!

It's important for you to appreciate the validity of Genetypes and how very real they are. You will see as much for yourself in Part Two when you identify people you know, but finding *your* true self will require faith in the process because your ego (nurtured, false self) will be working hard against you, protecting the mental models its worked so hard on building since your birth. The labels and limitations it gives you are about to be shattered! So permit me a further explanation of our ancient past and how Genetypes came to exist.

My work on Genetypes began over a decade ago. My curiosity was spiked by how much in common human history has across the entire planet, because where there is commonality, there is a *pattern*, there is an answer waiting for a question.

Why, for example, in completely separate continents that thousands of years ago could have had no contact with each other, are there Mexican pyramids and Egyptian pyramids (with only 11 degrees difference in latitude between Cairo and Mexico City)? True, without our modern technology and understanding of engineering, a pyramid was ancient people's soundest way of making a structure reach up and touch the heavens. But *why* did they all want to "touch the heavens" all over the world, much like the more recent Christian cathedrals do? Pyramids on both the continents have a similar arrangement of chambers and tunnels underneath them, and are aligned in some way with the sun, moon, or stars. Dismissing Egyptian pyramids *exclusively* as tombs is like saying medieval churches are tombs because they contain graves. A pyramid is a ludicrously ostentatious tombstone, even for a pharaoh! These pyramids were both clearly religious focal points and observatories (some Egyptian pyramids off the beaten tourist trails are open ceiling).

I was also stunned by the underlying commonality between Native American, Catholic, Hindu, and Arthurian stories—essentially the same plotlines told differently. Both ancient Mayan and Vedic cultures believed in the same 26,000-year cycle of light and dark ages despite these civilizations being on different sides of the world, the same calendars synchronized and most recently ending in 2012 to indicate a new age (not the end of the world).

This ancient global commonality also drew the interest of famous scholars and philosophers decades before I was born. As Franz Boas lamented, "There can be no doubt that in the main the mental characteristics of man are the same all over the world. Bastian was led to speak of the appalling monotony of the fundamental ideas of mankind all over the globe."

In 1916, a psychoanalyst named Carl Jung offered an explanation for this "appalling monotony" that also explains why and how our *individual* nature is both inherited and ancient (emphasis mine): "The collective unconscious comprises in itself the *psychic life of our ancestors* right back to the earliest beginnings. It is the matrix of all conscious psychic occurrences, and hence it *exerts an influence that compromises the freedom of consciousness* in the highest degree, since it is continually striving to lead all conscious processes back into the old paths... .... This collective unconscious does not develop individually but is *inherited*. It consists of *pre-existent* forms."

Sigmund Freud concurred with Jung's thesis in that he had cited "archaic remnants" in his subjects' minds, mental images that could not be explained by anything in the subjects' lives. Jung described the phenomenon as "*imprints or momentous or frequently recurring situations in the lengthy human past.*"

Jung argued that however much humans try to repress this link with "archaic remnants" in their minds, these remnants would find a way to surface regardless, albeit through different means. He later argued that the UFO hysteria of the 1950s—visits from gigantic circular objects in the sky (like the stars ancient peoples worshipped from their pyramids) was an ancient belief in a messianic encounter simply resurfacing in a new form. I would add that the UFO hysteria began as early as 1947 with the Roswell incident, perhaps an unconscious attempt by society to reunite with its stellar-worshipping past as a reaction to the fledgling and staunchly patriarchal postwar order.

So what are these "archaic remnants" lodged in our modern subconscious, these *"inherited pre-existent forms* from the psychic life of our ancient ancestors"? The answer to this question goes far further back in time than when Mexican and Egyptian pyramids were built, the Mexican pyramids only representing the *ending* of an older story. To understand our nature as an individual as well as a species, to appreciate where Genetypal life maps may have originated, and to solve the ancient mysteries previously pondered, we must rewind two and a half million years: to the dawn of humans in East Africa.

The Entity Inside You

Go back far enough, and we are all African immigrants. Millions of years ago, we migrated out of Africa and spread out into the Eurasian continent, splintering off and evolving into different species of humans: Neanderthals in Europe, Homo erectus in Asia, and Homo sapiens in Africa, to name the major ones, all existing simultaneously to begin with. And this was only the first great migration in human history. For the vast majority of human existence, we have been nomadic. Even when we had migrated and settled a region, we continually moved around within it as foraging tribes, or "hunter-gatherers," rarely settling a camp for long. Millions of years later, approximately 70,000 years ago, something triggered Homo sapiens to migrate out of East Africa, and recovered artifacts indicate that this trigger could have been finding spirituality, born of what we refer to as The Cognitive Revolution of our species. In short, the size of our continually growing brains seemed to reach a critical mass, and we suddenly acquired the ability to think, create, and wonder.

The common, scientific, and therefore solely logical explanation for the trigger of this Great Migration is given as food supplies dwindling in the face of growing population. That may certainly have added a push factor, but the food scarcity theory doesn't explain why the migration spread out so far and wide for such a relatively small number of humans, and why it became so daring a quest. This is because logic inevitably discounts the emotional side of the human brain—*the side that drives us.*

So what could have been the cause of that second Great Migration besides possible food scarcity? Imagine living on this planet without the knowledge we have today: that it's a sphere circling a sun in outer space. All you know is the patch of dirt you currently forage in. But then, around 70,000 years ago with the advent of The Cognitive Revolution, you suddenly start making observations and asking questions. Gigantic fireballs continually launch in the east, giving us light, warmth, and life until they land in the west, leaving us perpetually hoping a new fireball will launch after the subsequent darkness and cold. As we watch and wait for the next fireball (what we now call "sunrise"), we stare up at a sprawl of twinkling lights against blackness. Perhaps this multitude of lights are where humans' life energy goes when they die and where it comes from when they are born. The heavens seem to be in control of our fate. Perhaps we could find the source of these fireballs, these givers of new life, perhaps we could find and touch… our Creator. Let us begin a quest to find where these fireballs rise and fall, no matter what the risks or where it takes us, for we need to know our place in this world. What's beyond those "forbidden" mountains? Let's find out.

As Homo sapiens headed east, toward the rising fireballs, and entered Eurasia, they encountered a visibly alien humanoid species (taller, bulkier, and blue-eyed) who were, unbeknown to these Homo sapiens, their ancient relatives the Neanderthals who evolved after the first migration out of Africa millions of years earlier. This cataclysmic encounter could illustrate the dawn of Genetypes. I refer to "humans" in this book purely because Homo sapiens is the only human species to not be extinct; as we know, only Homo sapiens prevailed, and the other species died off. What happened?

There are only two theories offered as to why only Homo sapiens prevailed, and they are hotly contested: conflict or interbreeding —more black and white thinking. Couldn't it have been a little of both? One to four percent of some present-day Homo sapiens DNA was discovered in 2010 to be of Neanderthal origin. This could only be Neanderthal grandmothers' sapiens-diluted legacy, indicating at least partial interbreeding. It's also hard to imagine there was no conflict as these visibly different species encountered each other and fought for food supplies and shelter, but evidently nor was Homo sapiens out for genocide.

For our purposes, all we need to know is that Homo sapiens conquered the other human species, genetically and/or violently, *and that means they had some kind of edge.* I theorize that this edge illustrates the birth of the "inherited, pre-existent forms" I call Genetypes.

What was this edge of Homo sapiens? Neanderthals were physically bigger and stronger than Homo sapiens, and stereotypical beliefs of them being the proverbial dumb cavemen simply aren't true, so lack of brain or brawn cannot be the reason for their defeat. Homo sapiens garnering a belief in a religion could have transformed a rabble into an army, and a fearless army at that if it promised an afterlife. But uncovered artifacts provide evidence of Neanderthals also finding spirituality (skeletons respectfully buried with items deemed as needed for an afterlife), so what was the cause of sapiens prevailing over Neanderthal?

The clue to answering this question is that Neanderthals tended to hunt *alone*, whereas these African immigrant Homo sapiens, though smaller bodied, *worked as a large team*; a well-coordinated and overwhelming force is the only explanation for this victory. Violence, whether defending or attacking, is the hardest human activity to coordinate, but cooperation is the secret, and that necessitates *giving different people different purposes in the tribe*. This idea is key to explaining the origin of Genetypes.

Albeit a gradual process over thousands of years, for what was essentially a swath of forager tribes migrating out of their home territory on foot into strange lands with their families in tow and wielding primitive weapons, genetically and/or violently conquering the physically superior Neanderthals on their home ground was an astounding feat. This triumph could best be explained by the edge of superior organization skills that allowed them to cooperate in large numbers and/or genetic mutation choosing Homo sapiens over the other species. Either way, this is the earliest example of The Energy Field rewarding social skills over physical strength, an attribute more inherent in females than males, and we will come back to this point later. It doesn't take aliens or mysterious technologies to build pyramids, just social skills in the form of organizational hierarchies driven by a unanimous and fervent belief in something greater than ourselves.

Over the tens of thousands of years that followed, Homo sapiens didn't stop at Europe; they spread out into Asia, conquering Homo erectus before eventually even crossing *open water* to colonize Australia (Aborigine remain their closest descendants), and walking from Siberia to Alaska (The Ice Age made it possible to walk across The Bering Sea) before colonizing the entire American continent (Native Americans and Amazon tribes their closest descendants). There was plenty of land in Asia to spread out on and feed on without the need for daring sea voyages to Australia, weakening the argument of food scarcity being the *sole* reason for the migration.

I contend that Homo sapiens became the sole human species as a result of being a structured and co-coordinated society compromised of individuals *each with a defined purpose*, all bonded by a collective cause: a stellar-religion that was passed on to their descendants wherever they settled, hence the pyramidal observatories on both sides of the world. To function so effectively, this societal structure would've required a human chessboard of matriarchs and patriarchs, generals and warriors, protectors and priestesses, mystics and medics, scientists and storytellers, nurturers and youths, all working together and respecting one another's role.

This is how and why Genetypes were formed: a set number of specific tribe member roles continually imprinted on human DNA for at least 70,000 years, possibly even for the 2.5 million years that humans have existed. This surely counts as the *"imprints or momentous or frequently recurring situations in the lengthy human past"* that Sigmund Freud spoke of, and is therefore a likely explanation of how Carl Jung's *"pre-existent forms"* came to exist.

My Genetypal Theory builds on Jung's work with the benefit of genetic science and a decade-long endeavor to fully flesh out the Genetypes in a way that contemporary individuals can easily find themselves, their purpose, and hence, their new life map. Over the past six years, with thousands of people from a cross section of societies and backgrounds, I've conducted a multitude of trials and focus groups in different countries, testing and honing the theory, and the results have continually astounded me as much as the subjects. I would send the group to take an hour to study the Genetypal blueprints, and 100% of the participants would return with a shocked expression on their often-tearful faces as they held up their Genetype profiles.

How can these Genetypes exist within us after so long, bearing in mind how different our modern society is to those ancient times? Genetic mutation moves at a snail's pace, but society in the last few hundred years has moved at a leopard's pace, so our ancient genetic nature hasn't had time to adapt to this sudden modern environment. The relatively far slower pace of genetic mutation struggling to adapt to rapid modern society change is a condition I refer to as "genetic inertia." Genetic mutation isn't a speedboat; it's a sluggish supertanker with an undersized rudder. Turning the wheel hard to port isn't going to do a thing for a very long time because of inertia, just as the past few hundred years (0.012% of human existence) of modern life mutation and our divided society's whimsical wish list isn't going to budge 2.5 million years of ancient life mutation in a flash, if at all. We should of course turn the wheel, but we need a plan while we wait for this genetic supertanker to escape inertia, a plan we can execute within our lifetimes, a plan that ensures our species will survive.

Because of genetic inertia, it stands to reason that these various "tribe member role genes" are still skipping around in our contemporary gene pool. Even the last 1,000 years out of 70,000 years is a mere 1.4%, so for 98.6% of Homo sapiens dominance we've had various tribal roles continually imprinted onto and cloned into our DNA. The Genetypes this process creates still inhabit our subconscious, whether we like it or not, so we must align with these roles and adapt them to the modern day to become effective, whole, and happy. This is your nature; this is your personal truth.

These set, ancient tribal roles surreptitiously but doggedly tug at our present-day psyche through our "gut instincts." In a sense, you have been here before and shall be here again. Now we must discover exactly what you once were and what's *still* living inside you. We must reveal your Genetype.

Their Legacy, Your Legend

After the source of those "fireballs" (the sun) forever moved away from the migrating ancient ancestors' horizon, after coastlines continually deflected their course, their quest to find meaning and a Creator ended in agrarian servitude centered around civilizations run by elites who demanded the ultimate sacrifice. But through genetic inertia we are still explorers at heart, still searching for our meaning. Today, we may not be living in agrarian servitude, but we are living in urban servitude centered around shopping malls. We used to gaze at the horizon; now we gaze at celebrity magazines. Our Global Tribe has lost its way and must break free of this deadlock. Winston Churchill once said, "The empires of the future will be the empires of the mind." Let us heed his advice and continue the human adventure that those before us began.

Your ancient ancestors' legacy forged the plotline of your as yet untold story with their Genetypes still ingrained and scattered among us, waiting for you to recover yours, to unleash its power and drive your story and our story forward.

To successfully cross the map of contemporary human happiness will next require a Rite of Passage—a battle between nature and nurture, between your true *biological* self (made of genes) and your false *biographical* self (made of ego). From the Christian *book of Revelation* to *The Tibetan Book of the Dead*, this same inner battle has been encoded in different ways at different times under different skies because of shared ancient wisdom from long ago. Like the serpent, we must shed your outer layer of skin to find your inner meaning, and only then, with your true self driving, can you *truly* find everything else you desire in life; Purpose, Love, Health, and Money are the waypoints on our map.

Let us gaze at the horizon once again, the horizon of our *minds*. Let us embark on a quest to find your "spots."

part two

RITE OF
PASSAGE

Search and Rescue

"Maybe the journey isn't so much about becoming anything. Maybe it's about unbecoming everything that isn't really you, so you can be who you were meant to be in the first place." – Paulo Coelho

"Just be yourself," you are often told, and rightfully so, but how can you *truly* be yourself if you don't know who you are? Better advice is "Know thyself," but how can you accomplish that? The Law of Attraction says you can have anything you focus on, but how do you know *what* to focus on? There is no shortage of profound and useful self-improvement advice out there, but there is a missing piece of the puzzle that I am about to give you by unequivocally answering the questions that soul-searching humans have asked themselves for thousands of years: *Who am I, and why am I here?* Why you're here is a function of who you are, so our first step is to reveal your true self, your Genetype. Once you know your Genetype, who you truly are, your new life map will begin to materialize.

Answering the question of who you are is the most important event of your entire life. With this in mind, you may want to read this part of the book when you will have total freedom to focus. Over several years I have perfected this process, and I ask you to have faith in it and to trust your deepest feelings.

You are not reading a book for the duration of this part; you are engaging in a ritual. To live a functional life, a dysfunctional part of you must be severed, and this is the literary "knife" that will perform this ancient ritual in our modern setting. We aren't changing your

true self; we are recovering it. The only thing that must change is
the severing of false self, something that could terrify your ego. When
the book of Revelation talks about "apocalypse," this and its other
terrifying images are a metaphor of the battle for rebirth, of true
self versus false self. "Apocalypse" is derived from the Greek word
apocalypsis and translates as "lifting of the veil," just as you are
about to lift the veil on your personal truth, so light may conquer
darkness.

Hearing conflicting voices in your head doesn't make you insane;
it makes you human. This duality of the human condition has
inspired stories from *The Strange Case of Dr. Jekyll and Mr. Hyde* to
The Incredible Hulk. *The Lord of the Rings* eloquently portrays this
duality, especially through the character of *Gollum*, who refers
to himself as "we." Ancient storytellers said the same things on
cave walls.

Ancient artifacts show understanding of humans being comprised of two entities.
This section of a cave painting uncovered in Baja California Sur, Mexico, shows
female shamans conducting rites as well as human figures painted in light and
dark colors for different halves of the same person. Photo: James Sheridan

Ancient rites of passage were brutal by our standards: young teen boys physically separated from their mothers (sometimes for months) to have their foreskins sliced off with a flint knife, and to suffer ceremonial beatings, to name a couple, but they were appropriate for such dangerous times and served a purpose: "Look, blood. You're an adult now. Take your place in the tribe." Young females didn't need such a ritual because nature took care of that with their first period: "Look, blood. You're an adult now. Take your place in the tribe."

Today, females still get their first period, but males have no such rites, which is one reason why females mature faster than men and generally have spiritual stirrings long before males. But, even for a young contemporary female who has had her first period, that rite was merely the first layer of skin to be shed, and for the remaining stages she has little guidance. What we often risibly dismiss as a "midlife crisis" is actually our ancient genes stirring, telling us something is very wrong: that we are overdue for the next rite of passage, the one that progresses us from young adulthood to maturity, with a severance from everything our egos thought to be true. In short, it's about growing up.

Being raised by a single mother who didn't know where the next meal was coming from meant I had no such teen rites, but I found mine by chance in a different kind of tribe that used sticks as their "spears." Dashing around an ice rink from age thirteen led to a scout asking me if I'd like to play hockey for their junior team, and by age eighteen I wound up as a professional defenseman in Britain's premier league. Still not fully grown, I was thrown into an arena to battle with men who were older and heavier but who showed me no quarter for it. "Look, blood. You're an adult now."

It wasn't until I'd frozen an opponent's blood into home ice that my teammates and the fans would essentially tell me: "Now take your place in our tribe." But I still lacked "elders" to guide me through life, and I still had layers of skin to shed.

Our umbilical cord may have been cut physically at birth, but metaphysically, it remains in the form of what we refer to as "ego" and what I've identified with a false biographical self, or our *nurture*. This is also what Freud referred to as a "complex." From infancy, the ego builds mental models aimed at survival, such as don't walk off a cliff, don't touch fire, you're this, and you're that, often listening to elders for guidance as to its place in the world. It's trying to protect you *in childhood*. Entering adulthood, left unchecked by a rite of passage, ego becomes a separate entity that smothers your true self. Truth *will* find you at some point, but it could be too late. Eventually, your false self will die because eventually *you* will die. The trick is to ensure it hits the grave long before you do.

This duality—those "voices in your head"—between your true self and false self will sap your energy, cloud your judgment, and blockade your path to happiness. The voices in that corridor of life choices I explained in Part 1 have repressed your true self, buried it. But just as plants find a way to grow from out of the rubble to reach for the light, so does your true self. Truth will sweep away this rubble so we can reveal the beautiful plant that was quietly flourishing underneath. No matter what you've been through in life, there is a force inside you that has not and cannot be taken away from you because it *is* you. Its spirit is irrepressible and indestructible, and this is your search and rescue mission for it.

Passing the Gates

If you and I were alone together in a room, I could tell you your Genetype in under ten minutes, but without that luxury I need to prepare you for the common traps I've witnessed people fall into during my seminars, research, and consultations. So here are some hard-won tips before you pass the gates, to also jar loose the rubble that has fallen on the plant of your true self.

You're about to bump into yourself in the mirror, and you might not like it when you uncover some of what's been hiding there all these years. But that's okay. In fact, that's how you know you've probably found yourself, and we all have inherent flaws, as you will soon see. Imperfection is what makes us human. Don't let a mismatch between self-perception and your Genetype's profile throw you off the scent of truth.

I'm about to present you with the seven female Genetypes and the seven male Genetypes. Feel free to read both sexes, and perhaps you will recognize other people you know along the way. It's not fashionable to separate males and females, but it is a biological fact that the two sexes are simply born with different chromosomes, and recall that I'm focusing on your *biological* self. The other reason for dividing into sexes is to make it quicker for you to identify your true self; this way there are only seven to choose from instead of fourteen. Sex is separate to gender or sexual orientation, so please put these aspects to one side because I am not making any political statements here or trying to secretly replace broken panes of glass in the ceiling! Nor does this division into sexes attempt to portray females as having less important roles than males as you might *suspect* of our ancient past. As you will see, the truth is quite the opposite. Identifying your Genetype is merely a means to end: to derive your purpose in life, to make you happy. If the shoe fits, then ignore the social narrative *du jour* however much your true self contradicts it. Political correctness, by definition, is nurture and, not to discount its function, has no bearing on your true self.

Finding your Genetype can surprise you in that it's a fully formed alternative belief system to the one you might currently use. The trouble with such a "shock and awe" tactic is that it can trigger fear (your ego's inbuilt defense system), so don't be surprised if you involuntarily slam this book shut when you find yourself. That's just your ego realizing it is about to lose the game and running off with the soccer ball before the final whistle can be blown, like a child. Simply return to the page later on with a glass of wine as your wingman, and finish what you started, because you were most likely on the path of truth. Truth doesn't care about being popular, but it will set you free.

Dogma deafens, so be mindful of your thoughts as you search for your Genetype. Please read this notice carefully because it's not only for show; it's based on years of working with people:

EVERYONE HAS A GENETYPE. EVERYONE. IF YOU FAIL TO IDENTIFY YOUR GENETYPE OR CHOOSE THE WRONG GENETYPE, I GUARANTEE IT WILL BE BECAUSE YOU DIDN'T READ THE FOLLOWING BRIEF-ING CAREFULLY BEFORE READING THE PROFILES!

The most harmful lies are ultimately the ones we tell ourselves. This first point is the biggest trap people fall into: *wishful thinking*. Our perception of ourselves is rarely based on reality. Be careful you're not saying to yourself, "That's not who I am" when in fact you should be saying, "That's not who I *want* to be!" Also, *don't align your current or desired vocation with what you see in a certain*

Genetype profile. You must become a blank page for this exercise. For example, if you're a writer or wish to become one and you come across a Genetype that seems to obviously have the purpose of being a writer, that does not mean you have found the right Genetype! But nor should you rule it out. *Ignore what you want to be true.* You must empty your mind and open it fully for this process to work.

Stay focused on the imminent goal, which is *purely to identify your Genetype.* If another Genetype profile appalls you, don't get hung up on it, simply move on and worry about your own Genetype before those of others.

Ask the person who knows you the most *and who is not afraid to point out your flaws.* Parents and long-term partners are often adept at finding Genetypes of those close to them. I've witnessed this many times in focus groups and seminars where couples attended. *Just be sure it's done in a constructive way,* appreciating that we all have flaws.

Don't latch onto the first tiny detail that you identify with. For example, if you're an animal lover, don't simply pick the Genetype that appears to love animals. It's about getting to the core of the Genetype, the sum of *all* the parts.

Your Genetype shows up when under pressure. Something a crisis teaches you is that your true self shows its face under pressure, so a good test of the Genetype you think you are will be to reflect on how you acted under pressure in your past. Under the most pressured human circumstances, such as prison life or being a stranded survivor of a crash, true selves surface and prevail as humans uncannily default back to a natural organizational structure, because our ancient genes kick in when it counts most.

Read with your soul, not your head. Suspend skepticism and judgments. You're not writing a book review; you're trying to discover yourself. If this quest goes south, I guarantee it will likely be because you used your head instead of your soul. For the reader who has a high opinion of their intellect, for now, *let it go.*

Don't be tempted to figure out possible ancient Genetypal roles so that you can choose the character you want to be in an ancient screenplay. Each Genetype profile has a number of sections that I've perfected to be in a certain order designed to communicate with your true self and to dodge your constantly judging, comparing, and insecure ego. It's vitally important you think objectively, so I've refrained from giving each Genetype a name other than a simple code such as FG-7 (Female Genetype 7). By the same principle, I have not speculated on any tribal role each Genetype may have played in our ancient past, and I have portrayed each in our contemporary setting, not an ancient one.

Treat this as an elimination game. Cast out the "deal breakers" first, the Genetypes that couldn't possibly be you, *being honest with yourself,* and then zoom in on the remaining candidates. Be careful, though, not to hastily cast out your true Genetype just because you don't want to be that person! You may have to accept the one that is most like you, allowing the odd anomaly and being satisfied with a 95% match. Be *truthful,* and whichever Genetype remains, however bad it makes you feel or however "ridiculous" or "inappropriate" or "politically incorrect" or "so unlike you and your life" it seems, you have probably found yourself.

Don't identify only with all the good points of all the Genetypes. This is simply an attempt to ignore your inherent flaws. You'll find a *little* piece of yourself in *all* the Genetypes, but your *true* Genetype will have at least *one defining and dominant characteristic*, which you may or may not like. Follow the path in this direction, however bad it smells.

Expect to be torn between two Genetypes. This is common, but there will be something about one of them that doesn't ring true when you examine it in its entirety. Read them both carefully, casting aside wishful thinking. You'll perceive the wrong Genetype as more likable or "cooler" than the other, and you'll want this to be your Genetype. But ask yourself, which one of the two makes you (the false you) feel most uncomfortable? Which one scares you the most? That will probably be your Genetype.

In *Thus Spoke Zarathustra*, Nietzsche compares a child to a compliant camel who becomes a lion in adulthood, and this lion must slay a dragon called "Thou Shalt". You now stand at the threshold of the dragon's lair. Follow the path of truth, however rocky, and you will find yourself in the darkness.

Female Genetype 1 (FG-1)

Genetype summary:

You are the inherent compassion of The Feminine incarnate. You derive genuine happiness from nurturing, healing, and helping others. If you have children, they become your identity, even as they become adults. Motherhood and a sense of duty are what it's all about for you, but you could equally show the same compassion for a needy stranger as you would for your child. Nurturing others gives you pure joy, the bitter and the sweet this task carries. Self-ishness in others appalls you. You're "a ray of sunshine" to those you come into contact with, and "an angel" to those you care for. This dominant driver of your personality often means you have trouble refusing the distress calls of others, especially your children, meaning you can take on too much at once, and this can lead to stress, worry, and oversensitivity, as well as enabling those others to remain needy or to take advantage of your good nature (but this actually serves your purpose well, so you don't always mind). You don't see yourself as dependent, but your very nature makes you dependent on others so you can care for them.

How you've likely felt about this book so far:

Up until the part I asked you to look inward, you've been assimilating the information out of interest for people in general and what you can learn about *them* in order to help *them*, especially your children, but you felt uncomfortable any time I directed self-analysis at *you*. This is precisely because of your genuinely altruistic disposition, but it could be your undoing from the perspective of finding yourself. You may have snapped the book shut after the last paragraph or skipped this section to search for the Genetypes of others. Of all Genetypes, you struggle the most to admit this being you.

People say about you:

You're such a great listener, and kind and generous. You're deeply committed to your family, especially children. You perhaps prefer to stay home too much. Though you don't preclude the ideals, femininity and feminism are equally low priorities for you because you're too hyperfocused on caring for others, potentially to an unhealthy degree for both you and the recipient of your caring, though you would *never* concede this, and me even making the point perhaps irritates you. Those closest to you see a paradox: hanging above your radiant compassion is a persistent dark cloud, an inexplicable sorrow that some interpret as negativity.

Nightmares:

- Introspection
- Being helpless to protect your child
- Not being needed, being abandoned by those in your care
- Losing the child or patient in your care; your identity
- Being told that being overcaring is enabling the condition instead of fixing it

Not to be confused with:

FG-7 (she is partner focused, whereas you are more child/patient focused)

Female Genetype 2 (FG-2)

Genetype summary:

Enigmatic, wise, and in control of your emotions, you gravitate to the proving grounds dominated by males to show that you can do anything they can do, *only better*. You're a strategic thinker and a great judge of character, adding your female intuition to the often predominantly male team you fight for. You abhor anything that attempts to portray females as weaker than males or disadvantaged or different compared to them. You perceive that sort of thinking as holding you back and encouraging males to give you special treatment and handicaps. Compete, fight, and prove, you're a contemporary combatant in a concrete jungle. Fancy car, top hotels, and symbols of victory are required. You could accomplish any goal you turn your mind to. You're not competing with males to prove females are equal; you're doing it to show that *you* are *better than* equal, that *you* are the exception. And you often are.

How you've likely felt about this book so far:
You're a keen learner, always hungry for knowledge because you understand that knowledge is power you can use to *win*. The female Genetypes aren't nearly as interesting to you as the males, and you likely study the male Genetypes to scan for people you know so you can forge alliances with them to get ahead in what you perceive as a male-dominated jungle. You prefer this use of the book far more than for introspection.

People say about you:
They see you as the professional you are: dressed to impress, efficient, and smart. They sense plans going on behind the stoic eyes, and they wonder if those plans involve them. Other females are either impressed by your ability to remain calm or are baffled by what they perceive is a lack of emotion, so they often try to loosen you up with partying. If other females could only see how much you could help if they were on your team, perhaps if they hired your services, then they would see your value. Others see you as competitive, and this can cause a strain on friendships, especially if your need to compete drives you to flaunt material trophies, but they don't understand that you mean no harm, that this is simply your nature. Females notice how unashamedly magnetized to powerful males you are, not always appreciating that you see this as a strategic move, and not necessarily to date them. But in any case, you really only care how males view you, "Father's Daughter" that you are.

Nightmares:
- Losing at *anything*
- Not being accepted as "one of the boys"
- Betrayal or rejection by your team
- Being given special treatment at work for being a female

Not to be confused with:
FG-5 and A-Type Nurture (explained in following section)

Female Genetype 3 (FG-3)

Genetype summary:
You're a free spirit, sensitive to energy, other people, and animals. You're immune to the material trappings that tempt most other people, and you enjoy simplicity. This sensitivity to energy also means you can feel the pain and fear of others, and this can be too much for you to bear, so you often withdraw from life and public to escape it. Otherwise you'll try to please everyone in an attempt to ease their suffering, often becoming a "chameleon" to keep The Energy Field undisturbed, but when you do this too much you snap. Marriage and children aren't off the table, nor are they a priority. You often require solitude, and a place to call home is your anchor. You're the first person in a group to show interest upon presentation of a Ouija board, tarot cards, or astrology charts. Your connection to The Energy Field blesses you with the gift of creativity. You take pleasure in preparing and presenting a meal in your home for family and friends. Eager to listen and empathize but not easily swayed or pressured by other Genetypes, resolute wholeness and abstract wisdom waits for activation beneath your endearingly kooky demeanor.

How you've likely felt about this book so far:
You're intrigued and enthralled by the possibility of a personality blueprint being handed down from an ancient past. You sense that we are somehow not alone, that some kind of energy exists and flows through the universe and between people, so you're immediately attracted to anything that might explain and enhance the rich inner world you love to retreat to.

People say about you:

They sometimes wonder if you're smoking something, but they love you for it anyway. Sometimes you might actually be smoking something because you could see drugs as a way to open gateways to The Infinite and to silence the pain of others you sense and feel. Your leisurely and linear pace can sometimes infuriate others, but you won't be rushed, and you'll have a smile on your face, regardless. They wonder how you remain so calm and unaffected by modern life and trappings when they are so stressed, and they envy and admire you for this, not appreciating how much of other people's problems you can take on underneath that tranquil veneer. Literally or figuratively, you're the proverbial woman who lives alone in the woods, growing herbs and playing with animals, a gypsy, a kind witch. Unadulterated beings, such as children and animals, gravitate to you, sensing your deep connection to The Energy Field.

Nightmares:

- Loss of the ability to access solitude (not freedom as much as solitude)
- Disconnection from the spiritual world
- Loss of your home, your escape, your private space
- The Rat Race and material trappings
- Someone else controlling you, keeping tabs on you, confining you

Not to be confused with:

FG-6, FG-5

Female Genetype 4 (FG-4)

Genetype summary:

You glide across the room, oozing femininity and pheromone, both male and female heads turning in your wake as you gracefully conceal the power and joy that being the center of attention brings you. You know their convenient stereotype of "bimbo," but you also know the truth is quite the opposite—that you're an intelligent, strong-willed, and very creative woman, but you keep that to yourself because your effortless sexuality is already too much for most people to handle, especially females. They don't need to say as much because you can read body language and sense it, expertly wearing a stoic face so nobody knows you know what they're thinking. You do want the world to recognize you, though. You could be many things if you'd only see them through, but the fun is in the creating, not so much the completion. You're a born actress who loves the spotlight and camera, and the spotlight and camera love you back; there's a star-quality energy about you. But there's a paradox in this paragon: you enjoy the thrill of the chase as much as the idea of finding the perfect partner. Let the games begin.

How you've likely felt about this book so far:

You've quickly and merrily identified yourself here. The creative side of you appreciates the concepts presented so far, and if you've been confused about the unprovoked animosity from other females you've endured your whole life, then you've felt a weight lift as you learned why and that it's not personal. You care about your relationships, and you'll study the Genetypes with a view to being able to manipulate them.

People say about you:

Your ears have been burning for millennia, but there's no such thing as bad publicity, right? Females often feel threatened by your sexuality, instantly becoming territorial over their partners from seeing you as a predator, a husband-stealer. It's convenient for females to brand you as a slut/bimbo/jezebel/harlot/femme fatale or plain "bitch," but, yawn, that's something you've had to deal with since childhood, only now you can perhaps understand why. Other females don't understand the power you have over men, they assume it's just men being "gawking pigs." You inspire others to explore their sexuality and embrace it, not suppress it.

Nightmares:

- Losing your looks (despite age making this an inevitability)

- Rejection of any kind

- Having your sexuality compromised in any way

- Losing the spotlight

Not to be confused with:
FG-6. Caution: do not fall into the trap of *wanting* this to be your Genetype.

Female Genetype 5 (FG-5)

Genetype summary:
You are fearless and focused, capable of achieving a multitude of goals with vigor. But what it's really about is independence and equality for all, protecting those who need protecting with pen or sword, standing on the wall between the vulnerable and those who would oppress them. It's as if you're on permanent standby, poised to strike at threats to the weak, the minority, or the vulnerable. You may have an androgynous and/or Amazonian appearance, sometimes straddling the line between the masculine and the feminine, but not detracting from your attractiveness, leaving you occasionally uncertain about where and how you fit in with

society. You're not particularly concerned with the latest fashions. You probably have good hand-eye coordination. You're not the stay-at-home type, and you likely appreciate nature and the planet, especially exploring and protecting it. Being the sole guardian heroine can be a lonely affair, and other Genetypes often don't appreciate what a debt they owe your type and how much work still lies ahead for you.

How you've likely felt about this book so far:
If you're concerned about a white male author stereotyping women, segregating females from males, and/or covertly attempting to roll back women's rights by reverting to an ancient past and clinging on to patriarchy in the process, congratulations, you've likely found your Genetype. Important: I know you're worrying about how the other female Genetypes are portrayed here—that's your nature— but *please only focus on your Genetype.* You're a force for change, so you may have a problem with me saying not to change who you are, but an awakening to your true self is more profound and lasting than any other kind of change.

People say about you:
It depends on who is saying it. The Female Genetypes that need protecting the most will be grateful for your protection and can make good friends even though they won't identify with the causes that you do, unless it suits a particular agenda of theirs. Most females are stunned at the fact that you won't be afraid to walk down a dark alley at night, and they admire this fearlessness and how self-sufficient you are. They sometimes see you as distant, not appreciating how determined and singular you can be about goals and how serious your role as protector can be, the protection that granted them the freedom and safety they enjoy. But also, in your furious protection of the "villagers," they see you as sometimes blinded to the danger of burning down the "village" in the process.

Nightmares:

- Losing the ability to fend for yourself and to protect yourself from danger

- Not being able to protect a woman or child who was in danger

- Losing at anything, not being equal to or better than others in anything

Not to be confused with:

FG-2, FG-3

Female Genetype 6 (FG-6)

Genetype summary:

Forever young, inside and outside, you don't let the daily drudgery of life get you down, happy in your innocent bubble. Being oblivious to the danger in the world gives you a sense of being immune to The Big Bad Wolf, it makes you confident, and it's seductive to others as you *appear* to have all the answers. A playful and innocent child in an adult's body, you want your friends to stay in "Never-Never" land with you, putting marriage and children on constant postponement. But the delightful childlike character often has the consequences of being dependent on others to make decisions for you and look after you, making you vulnerable to evil and wrongdoing. You often attract a protective friend because of this, like the characters in Ridley Scott's film *Thelma and Louise*, with you as *Thelma*. The best stories resonate with us because of believable characters we recognize from daily life, and your Genetype is unwittingly used frequently by writers because of the inherent suspense created by your innocence meeting insidious danger, from Dorothy in *The Wizard of Oz* to *Alice's Adventures in Wonderland* to *Little Red Riding Hood*.

How you've likely felt about this book so far:

Because of your carefree nature, I'd be surprised if you weren't only reading a book like this now because you've reached a point in your life where you realize you're "not in Kansas anymore" or can no longer afford to be in "Kansas." Either you've witnessed danger or the danger of being dependent on others. In any case, you're through the looking glass now, and you sense the need to grow and reach your full potential, to *awaken*. Ironic that in a book that makes its core message one of not having to change but rather appreciating who you are, your Genetype has change built in; change is the inevitable and irresistible part of your nature, and a great gift awaits you and The Global Tribe if you can muster the bravery required to stand on your own two feet (more in Part Three).

People say about you:

You're a free spirit, a joy to be around. You're naïve and aloof. It depends on which Genetype you ask and in what situation. You will attract friends who want to protect you as well as friends who want to be more like you, *all of whom* can sometimes become irritated by having to pick up the pieces. Your relationship with your mother is particularly important to you, and you will do almost anything to keep in her good graces. You're a partygoer and you crave attention. You're flighty, jumping on new trends, changing your image as frequently as you change your circle of friends and relationships. You live in the moment with no care for tomorrow, and you're unaware (and often protected from) the consequences of your actions or inactions.

Nightmares:

- Making your own decisions and becoming independent
- Your mother's disapproval and/or lack of support

- Loss of freedom, stuck in drudgery of life, being controlled
- Confronting The Big Bad Wolf you've always suspected is out there somewhere.

Female Genetype 7 (FG-7)

Genetype summary:

You're a matriarchal figure, a no-nonsense leader, and a "queen" who wishes to reign alongside another as equal partners. Tough and capable, you're a woman who requires respect and watches over her family and/or professional subordinates if you have no family. Your identity is wrapped up entirely in your family, especially your romantic partner; their career is your career, and you loyally stand at their side for better or worse. You are a champion of marriage and fidelity. If your partner was unfaithful, you'd blame the other party before your partner. If you chose a partner wisely, you idolize them. If you have yet to find The One or if you have lost your One, you would instead divert this energy into your children, or to your own corporation, or any form of surrogate family you could rule over and support. Once your partner is finally found, your previously plain attire is suddenly forsaken for a tasteful image that matches the needs of their career. You will fight for anyone who needs your strength, even if outside your family, especially a child. You keep a clean and orderly home. You treat your partner's family in equal stature to your own, and if your partner came with children from a previous marriage, you would love those children as if from your own womb. You're happy with a simple life.

How you've likely felt about this book so far:

You've particularly seen the value in this section that lists all the Genetypes because you've been searching for your partner and family members here so you can better support them, *or*, if you've yet to find The One, you now have the best guide map to find someone suitable. If you've been in an unhappy marriage, you may now also see that, horror of horrors, you married the wrong Genetype—a partner not best suited to live up to the demeanor you require of someone to idolize. You feel empowered by knowing everyone else's Genetype because it gives you a mechanism to better support the members of your family and reign as the omnipotent "queen" you strive to be.

People say about you:

However much others may complain about you butting into their business or being overly controlling, it's you they turn to for advice, and they love how you're always there for them when they need you. Additionally, they snigger about how much you idolize your partner or have such a devout quest to find them, yet they also secretly admire the tradition and romance of the notion. You make it your business to know everyone else's business, but that's a matriarch's job: to maintain order in the group by knowing who's doing what and passing judgment with your word as law.

Nightmares:

- Not finding The One or losing them once found
- Your partner ruling over you, above you, instead of with you and at your side
- Losing your family, and especially losing control over them

Not to be confused with:

FG-1 (she is child focused, whereas you are more partner focused).

A-Type Nurture (explained in following section).

Male Genetype 1 (MG-1)

Genetype summary:

Logic is your god. Many people focus on their professional life, but for you it *is* your life, and happily so. You're focused and driven, making you adept at accomplishing goals but more comfortable as management, freelance, or professional rather than going all the way to owner/CEO of a corporation/organization. You're the perfect wingman and a loyal senior manager. You act as if the organization you work for is your own, setting the bar for yourself and others, and making you the employee that organizations dream about. You're why they invented the Rolodex, and you're likely to take your business cards on vacation. You are strategic, a logical planner, and a team player. A map of cause and effect guides your path, making the game of life seem obvious to you. Smart, orderly, and wise, you are the backbone of today's organizations.

How you've likely felt about this book so far:

You likely and rightly saw this as useful for marketing, recruitment, training, management, and your own personal advancement. When you get to the next parts of the book, you'll be reading with a view to understanding people in your organization rather than understanding yourself. You want order, making you motivated to settle disputes, and you'll likely see this book as a good tool for making sides see common ground and to understand that we are all different with different needs, often emotional based, as hard as that may be for you to swallow.

People say about you:

People look up to you at work, your superiors respect you, and competing organizations headhunt you. You can be competitive in a calm and healthy way, provided that arrogance doesn't creep into the exchange. You're sometimes perceived as fake if you schmooze too hard, but people also expect a degree of that in the corporate world. They like how you don't threaten them by not standing out too much in the workplace; you integrate and blend with the team. The opinion of people in the professional world is all that's relevant to you, so all is well. In your personal life you can be seen as lacking spontaneity and passion, somewhat withdrawn and robotic. Your family wishes they could feel closer to you, wanting you to let your hair down more, express emotions, and to not be so rigid or even pompous. More spontaneous Genetypes can feel very confined around you. You struggle to relax and be on vacation. But when faced with a situation, family members are reminded of how you can be counted on, always there for them with the wisdom of Solomon, keen to assist with your skills and knowledge.

Nightmares:

- Chaos, lack of structure and routine

- Losing your job or ability to do it; losing respect from colleagues

- Emotions of yourself or others, dealing with overemotional people

- Retirement, stillness

Not to be confused with:

A-Type Nurture (explained in following section).

Male Genetype 2 (MG-2)

Genetype summary:

Driven by a need for knowledge and understanding of the world, you require solitude to reflect and be alone with your thoughts. And the more you know of the world, the more you feel the need to withdraw from it; the drama, the hypocrisy, the brutality, the superficiality, it appalls you. You see what a long way the species still has to go, and you worry the malaise will burn you up, so you take refuge in your home. Your home is your castle, your laboratory, your watchtower, your bunker, and it's where you want to spend most of your time. If some kind of drama forces you to step out of your reclusive lifestyle, trouble can lie ahead, but you're happy to leave the home to travel to strange new lands, to learn and explore. You sense there is something else out there, perhaps other dimensions, and spirituality appeals to your nature. You're an intelligent and particular man who loves to read and to live inside your head, but the combination of this and your solitude can lead to disconnection from reality and to eccentricity, so you struggle with balance and the paradox of withdrawing from what it is you're philosophizing about.

How you've likely felt about this book so far:
There's a paradox in how you want answers, but if you found them the quest would be over, and you live for the quest, so it behooves you to retain an aftertaste of skepticism in any study. You could see this as a way to help you understand better why some people behave as they do, why they can sometimes be so annoying and illogical (to you). But this would require you to drop the skepticism that perpetually plays in the background and to actually apply the ideas instead of merely internalizing a theoretical critique.

People say about you:
They might see you as distant and aloof, even plain and unfashionable (not that you care about fashion), but that's because they don't have the opportunity of knowing you better. If they're allowed to peer into your sacred den, the average person might

see you as eccentric or weird and somewhat disorganized, but the people who would be *true* friends or lovers see an endearing cave of intrigue and would appreciate the multilayered individual you are. Those who are exposed to your philosophies and theories can have their lives changed forever, potentially drawing a great following or even changing the world. You shock people when they become victim to one of your rampages, which can take a personal and intimidating turn, as they previously wrote you off as a timid hermit.

Nightmares:
- Living among "the masses" and as one of them
- Loss of home and solitude
- Your inner monster letting rip
- Invasion of privacy, socially and legally
- Becoming totally detached from reality

Not to be confused with:
MG-3

Male Genetype 3 (MG-3)

Genetype summary:
Driven by creativity, you identify with your emotions, and these emotions sometimes overwhelm you; you lose control of them as if another entity has possessed you, especially if you aren't expressing them through a creative outlet. When that entity has departed, you wonder what happened and perhaps even what you said, often to those closest to you. But there is an upside equally as powerful, a blessing to match the curse: a vivid imagination, The Energy Field using you as a creative channel to speak through. You like to disrupt the status quo, indiscriminately challenge any

consensus, and wake people up. Passionate and spontaneous, intimidating and invasive, your eyes say it all: mysterious, intense, soulful, and ready to burn into foes, real or imagined. You probably like to wear loose or comfortable clothes before fashionable ones, ideally both. You sense a connection with energy and other dimensions, and you enjoy nature. Reflect closely on your childhood and what you loved doing and were good at, because your creative nature may have been long buried by societal pressure and ego.

How you've likely felt about this book so far:
You know you're unpredictable, but you secretly perceive this as power, keeping people guessing, nobody quite getting your number, so you're outraged to find me nailing your no-longer mysterious personality so precisely.

People say about you:
They sense the urgency underlining every word you say, as if your every exchange is life or death, animated and emphatic. Females can be moths to the flame. You're an intensely passionate and romantic lover, but potentially a jealous one, making you fly off the handle over nothing. Like an ocean, one minute you are gracing sailors with dead calm, the next you are a storm that kills them. In a society where males are supposed to conceal all their emotions apart from anger, hardly surprising that anger seems ever present to a degree in you; it's the only emotion of many for you that is considered acceptable for a male to show. You can be spontaneous and wild, heart of a party or a night out. Or you can be solemn and moody, dragging others into your personal apocalypse. But variety is the spice of life, or at least you tell yourself, seemingly oblivious to the chaos you leave in your wake.

Nightmares:

- Criticism

- Plagiarism of your work (if in a creative job)

- The Muse abandoning you (if in a creative job)

- Monotony

- The monster inside you devouring you and your loved ones, not only your enemies

Not to be confused with:
MG-2 and MG-6

Male Genetype 4 (MG-4)

Genetype summary:
You're immune to society's pressure on males to gain wealth and success, and you're too intrigued with *women* and partying to care. You don't need male friendships because women are preferred company for you. Most men love women, but not the way you do; you take it to a different level and from a different perspective. Women fascinate you, you see beauty in some form in *all* women, and you worship them. You embolden women and raise their self-esteem. Just because you relate to women so well doesn't mean you aren't masculine inside and out, and it has nothing to do with gender or sexual preference; you simply *love* women. This affinity and fascination with women makes you naturally do something that most other males can't or won't do: *you listen to them.* And that endears you to women, as does your sensitivity to energy; you can see into their hearts as other women can, you loosen them up, and you've probably been told you're psychic more than once in your life. You're a smooth-talking gentleman.

How you've likely felt about this book so far:

I feel like I've sold nuclear warheads to a rogue state by giving you the Female Genetypes, so please use responsibly. You'll care about the section on Female Genetypes more than your own, more than any other section in this book, only the chapter on love coming second place. You'd love the playboy lifestyle, but that requires wealth and success, and this often remains a pipe dream for you, so perhaps you're reading this book to better yourself financially or to set life goals, and I trust it won't disappoint. But you've also been intrigued by the idea of shunning fame and fortune in favor of finding your purpose in life because this principle aligns with your own and is refreshing to hear in this materialistic culture.

People say about you:

You're great to talk to, fun to be around, and often found laughing among a huddle of women at any party. You're sensitive, and that can make you changeable and suffer from mood swings, although always kind and gentle with women. Others, men especially, can see you as a dropout, a dreamer, or an anarchist, but they speak the language of patriarchy, and that is not your language. You don't follow rules happily, and some can find that frustrating. You just need a goal that aligns with your nature—we all do—but yours requires more searching to fathom. Depending on the female Genetype, the opinion of certain women will vary wildly.

Nightmares:

- Any event that deprives you of access to women
- Males seeing you as inferior, effeminate, or a "loser"
- Work, unless it involves partying with women (illuminating an ominous career option)

Not to be confused with:
MG-3 and MG-5

Male Genetype 5 (MG-5)

Genetype summary:

Forever young, carefree, and cocky, and if others want to grow up, that's their problem and their boring life, something they're reminded of when they come to you—a great friend—to unwind or find where the party's at. You prank and play, and you encourage others to loosen up. You have little interest in the trappings of life because that's exactly what they are to you: *trap*pings, and they represent responsibilities and commitments. Anything that would tie you down, even romantic entanglements, represent a potential threat to your freedom and playtime. Life is supposed to be fun, and you dress accordingly. The world is your playground, and children gravitate toward you for it. In fact, you have retained many aspects of your childhood, good and bad, while others lost them as they entered adulthood. A child is innocent, curious, loving, and fun. So are you.

How you've likely felt about this book so far:

You have the wonderful imagination and curiosity of a child, so you're excited about the possibilities and adventure of finding purpose, and you identify with the idea of that being more important than the mindless acquisition of wealth. You enjoy learning new ideas because you scramble to make sense of the world and create mental models for everything, so you see this as a useful handbook.

People say about you:

You have infectious enthusiasm, playfulness, and excessive boldness, often patting yourself on the back over a dubious or simplistic claim. You can be charming and mischievous, eavesdropping and telling stories, living in a fantasy world. When it comes to others trying to engage in a serious conversation with you, they wonder if they're getting through; you appear distracted, somewhere else, with a blank look on your face, and this can be frustrating. They're curious about your dress sense, sometimes seeing it as inappropriate or unprofessional, not that you'd care. You'll often either not make a major decision or consult with several people in order to make any major decisions. You're seen as a risk-taker with a sense of invincibility about it, parading like a superhero.

Nightmares:

- Loss of freedom, being tied down and trapped

- Being loaded down with responsibilities and commitments

- Becoming severely sick, elderly, or disabled

- Boredom, monotony, hard work, wearing suits or uniforms, and working in a cubicle; strictness and rigidly structured environments

Not to be confused with:
MG-4

Male Genetype 6 (MG-6)
Genetype summary:
In the moment, in your body, in the fight, you care little for tomorrow or career. You are a fearless protector who will readily take up a cause, although there is simple joy in a battle without a cause or even by rebelling against a cause. Fiery and quarrelsome, you walk through life on a knife edge, scanning for danger, sometimes secretly wishing someone would dare threaten those

you love so you could spring into action and mercilessly test your bodily skills. Most males loved Han Solo in *Star Wars*, but you identified with him most; you "prefer a straight fight to all this sneaking around." Diplomacy can only go so far, and you live for the moment they push the panic button so your phone will ring. Yours is the wrong house to break into, a truly bad day for the invader. Quick to the fists, sometimes too quick, actions are preferable to words. You can fly off the handle too easily, and this can lead to relationship issues. You are a very literal man, and life is simple for you: fight until the death. Your lust for guts and glory makes risk and action appeal to you. You're spontaneous and drawn to danger.

How you've likely felt about this book so far:

You want victory, so you will use this book as your spear and shield to compete and win at The Game of Life. There is little duality in you, if any at all. You have found yourself here, and you are proud to be this Genetype. This has confirmed and validated everything you suspected was true about yourself, only now it has definition. You may have scanned the other Genetypes for threats or opportunities to be victorious over anyone you see as an enemy. You want to ferociously protect your friends and family, so perhaps you will search for them here so you can see their weaknesses and better equip them for life's battles.

People say about you:

You're such a singular person, there are no surprises in how others see you, and you care little about what they say. The practical way you often dress reflects this indifference, preferring combat shorts or a utility belt over a suit. People sense itchy trigger fingers, and they can become quickly intimidated. You seem on edge, oversensitive to things people say or do, taking things too literally and overreacting, overly aggressive. You can sometimes appear uncouth, thickheaded, and animalistic, "such a guy," living for the moment. You can belittle other men when you sneer at them for not being "real men," so you often gravitate to the same Genetypes as you.

Nightmares:
- Disability
- Failing at defending those you love
- Losing any battle, especially physical
- Being a corporate "drone"

Not to be confused with:
MG-3 and MG-7

Caution: do not fall into the trap of *wanting* this to be your Genetype.

Male Genetype 7 (MG-7)

Genetype summary:
You are a tower of confidence and a Renaissance man, multitalented, always striving to be the best and to have the best. You *need* to be the man in charge, in both your professional and personal life, and anything other than first place is abhorrent to you. Anyone who challenges your power or position will incur your wrath, and justifiably so, you believe. Best friends or worst enemies? Others must make this choice when it comes to you, although when you say "best friends," you actually mean "loyal subjects." If family members don't regularly come to pay their respects *of their own accord*, they could be in danger of being financially cut off or excommunication or your disapproval. And if they show up when you've had to run out, you think that's too bad because you're an

important man. You care about your family but don't know how
to show them emotions and love—you see that as weakening your
power—so you use gifts to do the job, or a promise of something
in the future if you're broke, or your partner. You "rule" over a black
and white world, the masses "either with you or against you,"
embracing excess on an endless quest for more and more power,
and you often succeed, thanks to your aptitudes, confidence, and
charm.

How you've likely felt about this book so far:
You feel you are never wrong, so anything you read here that doesn't
correspond to what you believe will cause you to dismiss me as
a fool, someone not worthy to be in your "court." You have no
duality, which is what makes you a confident leader, so you don't
see anything wrong in what I say about you, even when I directly
point out your flaws. Your response will be to say, "Well, if other
people hadn't acted that way, then *I* wouldn't have to act that way."
You embrace the idea of not needing to change who you are because
you have no intention of changing.

People say about you:
It depends where you sit on the leadership-style spectrum, with
Mahatma Gandhi and Adolf Hitler as its two extremes. On the
Gandhi side: "I owe him everything. What an inspirational leader."
On the Hitler side: "He's a deluded and egotistical megalomaniac
who will never admit he's wrong. How can we humiliate him
and make him eat his words?" Now choose your *desired* position
on the Gandhi-Hitler scale, and you shall *choose* what people say
about you.

Nightmares:
• Being a king without a "crown"; you generally need money
  and/or power

- Losing control of everything and everyone, especially a daughter
- Disrespect; challenge of your power
- Showing emotions; you see emotions as weakness
- Losing to The Joneses

Not to be confused with:
A-Type Overlay (see next section).

Separating Nurture from Nature

"God does not play dice." - Albert Einstein

Welcome back. It may be initially difficult for you to accept who you truly are, but it is necessary if you seek an authentic life experience. It's about distinguishing between what is your reality and what is not, something Hindus and Buddhists refer to as *viveka* (discernment).

What obscures your vision when trying to find your Genetype is your nurture. These nurtures are like scratches on the surface of your true self, and we must polish them out. I've found the most powerful three nurtures that distract people from finding their Genetype to be Parental, Generational, and A-Type. To help you further consider your Genetype, let's look at each.

Parental Nurture:

Your parents are/were not God, but they obviously played a large part in your nurturing as a child, in the forging of your false self. At an unconscious level we aim to make our parents proud even in the cases when they clearly don't want to be proud, their own egos not wanting you to surpass them. Consider that your parents too had/have a false self, and that is the side of them that likely played a part in your nurture, perhaps projecting their own demons onto you. Unfortunately, many well-intended parents push children toward certain paths that are of the parent's liking, not the child's, and it's only 1 in 14 odds that the parent and child are the same Genetype, so each party probably has inherently different outlooks. Genetypes are evidently not inherited from immediate family, they are inherited from ancient ancestors, randomly skipping all over different generations. Children aren't supposed to be clones of parents; they are clones of the ancestors with the same Genetype. Recall what your parents wanted you to be, overtly and covertly, and maybe you're already doing it. Then be sure their voices aren't in your corridor, influencing your Genetype choice. At first, The Wizard of Oz was an intimidating figure to Dorothy, but it was only a *projection*. When her little dog pulled back the curtain, it was merely a scared old man (true self) hiding behind an illusion (false self).

The Generational Nurture

You'll have heard of "Baby Boomers," "Generation X," and "Millennials." What you may *not* have heard of is that these generations have a matrix of typical personality traits and that these generational nurtures are nothing new in history. "Millennials," "Gen-Xers," and "Baby-Boomers" are merely contemporary sound bites for personality types that have been here before, and, unless we break the cycle, shall be here again. To understand, permit me a brief sidebar, and this is something I'll refer to in the final part of the book.

Franklin Roosevelt said, "There is a mysterious cycle in human events... . . . this generation has a rendezvous with destiny." Then came Pearl Harbor. That was approximately eighty years ago as I write this in 2020. This was the last time we saw the climax of this destructive cycle, but let's go further back. Below is a list of other infamous climaxes in history and the dates of their duration:

War of the Roses 1449–1487

Spanish Armada Crisis 1569–1594

Glorious Revolution 1675–1689

American Revolution 1773–1789

American Civil War 1860–1865

World War II 1939–1945

Notice anything about the number of years between each of those cataclysmic events? It's approximately eighty years, fairly close to the length of a human lifetime. There's nothing supernatural going on here when you appreciate that generational personality types are involved. As the last generation to remember the horrors of war dies off, leaving nobody to warn or influence the generations that exist, we repeat the mistakes of our past. It's also caused by the boom-and-bust cycle that I'll touch on again in the next chapter, and how society evolves after wartime, in line with the parenting that reacts to it, swinging from one extreme to the other.

As Strauss-Howe Theory explains in *The Fourth Turning*, after a decisive war or cataclysmic event as those historical climaxes I listed, society swings to a rigid world that returns to traditional values, where the newborns get spoiled to compensate for their parents' neglected (depression and wartime) childhood, and this new generation of a new order have morals drummed into them. There's today's Baby Boomer. As those Baby Boomers reached adulthood (as well as rebelling against The New Order), they were relatively neglectful of their children and then were surprised when these latchkey kids became rebellious. The 1970s gave birth to a spate of horror films where children were demons, appealing to those Baby Boomer parents: *Rosemary's Baby, The Omen, and Children of the Corn*, to name a few. There's today's Gen Xers. As those Gen Xers reached adulthood (as well as rebelling against *everything*, further unraveling the conservative post-war values), they overprotect their children to make up for *their* childhood. There's today's Millennials. Our present cycle is summed up by the music transitioning from Monkees to Motley Crue to Mumford and Sons.

Here are the Generational Nurtures for Baby Boomer, Gen X, and Millennial. Each set of these false traits tends to affect how Genetypes come across, how they're "artificially flavored," but if you look carefully, the truth lies underneath this rubble. For example, an FG-1 is particularly selfless, but selflessness is also a typical Millennial trait, so female Millennials should be careful not to assume they are FG-1 Genetypes, while not ruling it out.

"Baby Boomer" born 1943–60

Typical attributes: Moralistic, resolute, creative, spiritual. Bombastic, narcissistic, presumptuous, ruthless. Principle-focused.

"Generation X" born 1961–81

Typical attributes: Street smart, practical, perceptive, survivalist. Individualistic, unfeeling, bottom line, amoral. Self-focused.

"Millennial" born 1982–02

Typical attributes: Selfless, rational, competent, idealistic. Lacking leadership, mechanical, bold, innocent. Community-focused.

Your *true* self is not a Baby Boomer or a Gen Xer or a Millennial. These historical-parental nurtures are just another potential smoke screen to finding your Genetype.

The A-Type Nurture

Certain people have what's called an "A-Type" personality, and you may have heard of this or already know that you're one. This is such a strong and resilient complex that it could lead you to believe you're certain Genetypes when you're not. When it comes to ego resilience, if normal ego is The Marines, A-Type ego is The Navy Seals. The ego is a force that tries to prevent you from finding your personal truth, as if to guard a fortress that imprisons that truth, so it's a much bigger problem when Seal Team Six are the guards. I suspect this complex is the result of the stronger-willed Genetypes becoming exposed to insecurity or chaos at a young age, resulting in unconsciously compensating for it later in life by trying to control everything, everyone, and every future event in The Universe.

Sadly, many A-Types don't *know* they're one and that there are others like them, and they've endured a world of apparent isolation where, for all their successes, they're constantly labeled with being over-controlling, bipolar, OCD, hyperactive, autistic, angry, you name it, when they're merely an A-Type personality. I don't know of any A-Type rehab clinics, but there should be.

So how do you know if you're an A-Type, to be sure you aren't letting this nurture blind you to finding your true self? Ticking all these boxes should raise the flag:

1. They don't procrastinate for long.

2. They are extremely goal-driven with a to-do list for every occasion, with several alarms set for different things.

3. They are arrogant, attacking perceived stupidity like a shark to blood in the water. This often means they cut people off in conversation.

4. No task is impossible; it simply requires the will to complete it. They simply don't understand the concept of laziness.

5. They possess laser-beam focus, and this is their key secret to success. They're also perfectionists; it's not only about getting it done on time.

6. Failure at any task is abhorrent to them.

7. They're worriers, trying to predict and control every possible outcome in life, brutally disappointed when the inevitable perfection doesn't turn out as expected. Sleepless nights are common. They have plans for almost everything.

8. They find it impossible to relax. Work is always preferable. They can eat a meal standing up or pacing.

9. Once they've found their right career, that's all they care about, relationships coming second place.

10. They love attention.

11. Dawdling is for losers; if you have to get somewhere, then move with purpose.

12. Tardiness is abhorrent for them, and they expect others to feel the same way.

Here are three more nurtures that must be separated from your nature, to help find your Genetype.

Political Nurture:
Of course you will have a political bias, but this is nurture by definition, and you must not let it get in the way. Everything is prepackaged for us today, and political parties are no different. It saves thinking. Let's assign the debate about who should be our next ruler to a different theater because politicians won't change your life anything close to how much *you can* at this very moment.

Nationality Nurture:
I spent 20% of my life viewing the world from 36,000 feet, and up there the planet appears as one rock, not fragments. As you now understand from our ancient past, these Genetypes are universal across the world, exposing geographical borders as haphazard partitions of the planet and its dominant species, nothing more. Examine what constitutes the values that your government imposed on you, the particular social narrative that's unique to your nationality, and segregate them from your true self.

Life Stage Perceptions:
Unless you're a very young reader, you will know that our attitudes change as we mature. Ancients understood that the human life cycle is, like so many cycles in nature, a *quaternity*. Four seasons, four weeks to a month and four quarters in a year, four stages to the lunar cycle and menstrual cycle, and four quadrants in religious symbols from crosses to swastikas. The four "seasons" of the human life cycle are: 0–20 Childhood (Spring), 21–40 Young Adulthood (Summer), 41–60 Maturity (Autumn), 61–80 Seniority (Winter). As we pass through these life seasons, the reality of mortality growing with each passing glance in the mirror, we tend

to *naturally* become more present, reflective, and humble (varying according to Genetype). We look back on our mistakes, the doors we mistakenly thought were locked, and we become less fearful of choices, walking the fine line between wisdom and cynicism. The flaws of your Genetype that I pointed out may no longer be apparent if you've matured past them, so don't let this throw you off the scent of your true self. Some Genetypes are success driven, like people in young adulthood. Some Genetypes are more spiritual, like people in seniority. Some Genetypes are more playful and carefree than others, like those in childhood. Know what stage in the cycle you're at, know what the other stages look like, and be sure this isn't distracting you from correct Genetype choice.

All these distracting overlays are the *nurture* dumped onto your inherent *nature*, the rubble on the plant, and we must dig out your soul to unveil your personal truth. If you think you found your Genetype, still keep an open mind as the book continues, and don't rule out the possibility you got it wrong. So stay here, engaging in this ritual as long as you need to, and *please don't read further until you think you've found your true Genetype!*

(If you're stuck and still unable to find your Genetype, you're likely still reading with your head instead of your soul, so here's a quick cheat and final word [and a repeat from the briefing]: *Get someone else to find your Genetype for you,* but it must be someone who's known you the longest and is not afraid to tell it to you like it is. And you must give them permission to tell you the truth without being sensitive and without you preselecting a shortlist for them to look at; they must see all seven Genetypes.)

Mark the date because today was your second birth, a *rebirth*. You have found yourself, the *real* you. You have answered the question: *Who am I?* You've evolved, you've leaped toward consciousness of thought and action, the quality that differentiates human animals from other animals. You also now know that you aren't alone in how you think and act, you aren't "crazy" or "bipolar," and there are millions more people across the world who are Genetypal clones of you (find them at Genetypes.com).

False self is like your shadow; you will never lose it, but now this entity is separate from you. Consider this cluster of complexes as a child clinging to your side, insecure and needy, reacting based on its fears and prejudices, waiting for a reassuring hug from you. There is a "deleted scene" in your biography, a painful event in childhood that was covered up in your memory, but when you remember it you'll understand that child beside you.

Now that you know *who* you are, you must know *why you're here*; we must dust off the life map that was hidden in your ancient genes, and craft your contemporary legend. Look, blood. Your false self has been severed. Next you will take your place in our Global Tribe by defining your purpose in it.

part three

BLISS BOUND

Destination: Bliss

"Why am I here?" Asking this question is somehow hardwired into our genes, and it represents a key difference between human animals and other animals: the *potential* for consciousness of thought and action. A more negative way we ask this question (often to the sky) is, "What's the point in it all?" or "Is this all there is?" but it's all really the same question being asked in different ways: "*What is my purpose?*" Implicit in *that* question is a belief that *we need to be of service to something greater than ourselves*, or why would we ask the question? We would simply get on with our selfish little lives as the rest of the animal kingdom does. And *whom* are we addressing this question to if not to something greater than ourselves? Who are we expecting to hear us? "What is my purpose?" is effectively the same as saying, "*How can I be of service?*"

Each Genetype has a gift to give The Global Tribe by living a life in accordance with its purpose. Recognition of this gift brings harmony within and without. Refusal of this gift brings destruction within and without. Sometimes we refer to this as our "calling" (which begs the question, "*Who or what is* calling you?"). The payoff for answering the question, "What is my purpose?" correctly is passage to the bliss state. Your bliss state is where both time and your mind are still, where you are at peace, and where your Genetype is naturally aligned with The Energy Field. Work is not work if it's meaningful. We don't watch the clock when time stands still. "Purpose" is what you were meant to *do* on a day-to-day basis, not *necessarily* as a job or for reward, and it involves a bittersweet balance because true love of anything is bittersweet. This isn't a psychological concept; it's a practical concept that leads to one, as an orgasm does. Where could this concept have come from?

For around 2.5 million years, our Global Tribe lived as nomads, spreading across the entire planet for the second time around 70,000 years ago, and this transient culture left few clues about it behind until humans formed the earliest civilizations such as those of ancient Egypt, our East African birthplace, where the symbols and scriptures laid bare tens of thousands of years of shared beliefs and genetic memory imprints, including polytheist religion. Multiple gods had multiple *purposes*—a goddess of war, a god of feasting, etc.—and were often evenly balanced between female and male deities. Indeed, the moral of the myths that surrounded these deities was most often about maintaining balance.

An ancient human might have proclaimed, "*I* worship The Goddess of Love," or "*My* God is Ares," often an individual or even an entire city focusing on one god or goddess as their patron. Effectively, we as individuals picked a deity that matched our personal needs or even our *personality and our purpose*, garnering what even today we refer to as having "a personal relationship with God." From the legacy of ancient Egypt, and what would be eventually handed down to Rome, ancient Greek civilization fleshed out the personalities of gods and goddesses in a colorful way, complete with elaborate myths to help define them, *and each of these deities' personalities had an uncanny resemblance to the fourteen Genetype profiles.* Did the gods of ancient Greece make humans in their own image, or was it the other way around; were those gods projections of ourselves?

(Sidebar: I won't reveal here which god or goddess your Genetype is identified with because I don't want to influence your Genetype choice, but if you've *definitely* found your Genetype, you can find them on a free download at www.JamesSheridan.com/omg.)

Before around 10,000 B.C., finding your purpose would have been a simple affair, especially once Genetypes and their gods had formed, because for most of our existence our individual purpose was based on a certain function within a tribe. Protectors would protect, nurturers would nurture, and shamans would tell stories from the other dimensions that spoke to them. Bring those ancient Genetypes into the present day, and it's not so easy and obvious (the shaman would probably be committed to an insane asylum). What changed?

Around 10,000 B.C., humans transitioned from a nomadic, foraging tribe existence into an agrarian one. We discovered agriculture and settled in one place, we gradually became hoarders and servants of the land instead of explorers of it. We began to live in houses and acquired possessions to fill it, we went to work each day, we developed our own agendas instead of communal ones, and we worried about the future and how the weather might affect our crops. Ten thousand years is a long time of living this way, but even that's only 0.4% of human existence and not who we are according to the principle of genetic inertia.

As agrarian settlements sprung up, so did the elites who offered law and order to "protect" them; rulers, artists, clerks, priests, and soldiers basically ran extortion rackets that left the new peasant class with less than when they were foragers. From then on, Genetypal purpose was steadily buried by society. Around 200 years ago (0.008% of human existence), The Industrial Revolution superseded The Agricultural Revolution, and what was left of Genetypal purpose was buried even deeper by society in the form of what we refer to as "The Rat Race," and everything and everyone in the culture participated in pushing us "rats" onto the starting line. Those ancient extortion rackets ran by elites to protect synthetic borders are what we now refer to as "taxation."

The constructs of relatively recent society are what now stand in the way of most Genetypes living their inherent purpose. If society stands between you and living your true purpose, then the present social narrative must be disregarded.

We are programmed to conform, for survival, hence why today we care so much what's "trending" on the Internet. It's possible that when you learn what your purpose is in this part of the book, society will laugh and say, "Who do you think you are?" This adversity can be discouraging. Before we consider exactly what your Genetypal-based purpose is, let's clear the path to it. How can we accomplish that? The same way we defeated your ego: by shining a light on it. You will answer back to society: "Who do you think *you* are?"

Who Do You Think You Are?

What *is* this entity we call "society" all about? What does it want us to do, and why are we trying to impress it so much? In the previous part, in the section on "Generational Nurtures," I explained the shifts in societal attitudes that cycle over and over on an eighty-year basis. What society wants us to do is a function of dates on a calendar, its mood frequently changing.

How many people are currently in jail for possessing or selling naturally growing plants (cannabis and marijuana) that society is now considering legalizing? In the aftermath of the 2008 financial crisis, how many families were "shamed" to have to live in vehicles or tents? Who shamed them instead of asking if that was a more fun way to live? If you think back even ten years ago, the social narrative was likely different to today, and if you challenged society about its rolling hypocrisy and whimsical nature, it might reply, "Well, that was then and this is now." Society is fickle. You might even say that society is a paranoid schizophrenic. Why should we worry so much about trying to impress an entity that can't seem to make its mind up and acts like a person who is mentally ill? We obviously have to obey its laws of the day (which also are a function of dates on a calendar), but why are we so stressed about conforming to it?

You've been nurtured to conform to society, to fit in, and this idea aligns with your true *nature* in your ancient genes because being part of a tribe used to be the only way to survive. "Herd behavior" sings to our ancient instincts. So, does modern society have any consistent message outside of The Ten Commandments? Yes, it does, because its message revolves around the "religion" that has sustained it for the last 200 years: consumerism.

Today's "herd" has been infected with a parasitic disease of compulsive and excessive consumption, chasing its tail as it fights a losing battle to find purpose. So few of us know our purpose in life that most people end up on the wrong path, working too many hours doing a job they hate. Then, because they feel so bad for selling their souls, they buy "stuff" as compensation for the trauma. Consumption is something we can define and control, unlike purpose, which is buried under the surface along with our true nature, and requires more effort to acquire than something shiny at the shopping mall.

We grovel for promotions at work, we provide running commentaries of our lives on social media hoping someone out there will be our "friend" or "like" us as a result, we distract ourselves with home makeovers and vacation planning, and we purchase material possessions such as houses and cars, not as much for shelter and transport but as if they are trophies to be flaunted as status symbols so that society will be impressed.

After playing hockey, in an attempt to conform more, I sought a career as a realtor in my early twenties, and the first thing I learned was, "People aren't buying a house, they're buying a life-style." What starts as a harmless "lifestyle" choice soon becomes a hunger for a *better* lifestyle than The Joneses. We are buying a lifestyle that disagrees with something in our DNA, the lifestyle we are *told* we want, and we are drowning in ludicrous debt levels to do so. We have been nomadic on a micro and macro scale for approximately 99.5% of our existence, and only for the last 12,000 years did we even begin settle into permanent abodes. Considering genetic inertia, perhaps this far lengthier nature pro-grammed into our ancient genes is why some people forever want to move houses, why some people continually live in renovation projects, and why we can *all* sometimes see personal residence ownership as a chain around our neck. When we weren't migrating, we were moving around in our local area as tribes of foragers. Our possessions totaled all we could carry. Maybe that's why today we feel that when we acquire too much "stuff" we feel as though the "stuff" owns us rather than the other way around.

We mindlessly lock onto every visual cue we feel will make us con-form to society with the least amount of effort, like a chimpanzee in training. The advertisers are our trainers, and they now have the power to expose us to more of these visual cues than ever, whether it be through a celebrity magazine, social media, video games, TV, or even books. The human brain is a comparing engine, so it continuously scans for reference points, to interpret the value or meaning of something. Notice how common it is to see the use of comparison in commercials. The actor can't simply look happy with what he has; the commercial must involve the actor getting respect from others because of the product he's enjoying. The advertisers know people a lot better than they know themselves, and they are winning a game that people don't even know they're a player in, especially young children.

Have you noticed how another car speeds up when you overtake it? Humans are competitive by nature. Putting a second mortgage on a family home to pay for a wedding, just to keep up with a societal trend to spend hundreds of thousands of dollars *on a party*? Our children committing suicide because they don't have as many "likes" as another kid on social media? This societal entity we constantly try so hard to impress is asleep at the wheel of a gas-oline truck, meandering toward a canyon. We tut-tut and shake our heads at the *nonsense du jour*, not once staring into the vanity mirror to wonder if we are the cause of this creeping horror, and we keep our foot to the floor, hoping that more of the same under a different brand name will finally give us a sense of purpose.

You will never beat the Joneses. Ever. I'm not being defeatist, only realistic. There will always be people who have more status, money, and power than you. Even if you did beat them, you would not truly have the satisfaction of beating them because they would never speak to you again, so the end result would not be the admiration you sought. There will always be a new carrot dangled in front of the donkey, but the donkey never considers if there's anything else to eat. Better off not being a donkey.

You must now rise above all the societal noise because you have a rendezvous with your true purpose in life, with your *higher self*. And the more people who do the same, the more chance there is that society will transform into something that isn't a ball of rambling contradictions with no universal core value of any meaning, rolling down a path to its own destruction. "Who do you think you are?" You know your Genetype, so you *know* who you are. Does society?

On Purpose

Now you must respect your Genetype by unapologetically defining its purpose in your own words. In short, it's time to own it. We are about to discover your destiny by revealing your purpose, and there can be no half measures in your sacred right to living it and delivering your gift to The Global Tribe. Discovering your true self is a clearance for action, not an excuse for compromise, *and you shall make no apology for who you are.*

We will shortly break out into a customized brainstorm for each Genetype. First let me offer some ideas and help you consider the potential distractions from finding your purpose:

Don't let ego get in the way.

We haven't terminated your ego by finding your true self. Like your shadow, your ego is ever present. The best we can do is to not identify with it, be mindful of it, and not let it blur your vision of truth. Allow your mind to take its natural course, and trust your feelings. If you find yourself choosing a purpose to impress others, you're probably identifying with ego and society instead of true self.

Focus on strength.

To respect your Genetype is to respect its flaws, and all the Genetypes have them. Focusing on *both* strengths and weaknesses as a whole tells you what your purpose is because your weaknesses tell you what your purpose is *not*. It's about deduction as well as selection.

For example, police work often attracts the MG-6 Genetype because of his natural propensity toward protecting and being where the action is, but is he the right man for this job, considering this Genetype is also fiery, quarrelsome, and quick to the fists, seeing everything as a threat? In ancient times this would have served warriors and hunters well, but not in contemporary police forces. This Genetype-purpose mismatch is the cause of the constant stream of police brutality outrages we witness today, and police departments would do well to include Genetypal awareness in their recruitment. Conversely, FG-5 (protect the vulnerable) and MG-1 (logic) are far better Genetypal matches for police work, but not so much for military duty.

Bliss is bittersweet.

Finding and living your purpose doesn't mean living a totally perfect life because *real* life is bittersweet, but it will be a life based on truth, consciousness, and lucidity as you do what you are meant to be doing each day, living in your personal bliss, without those nagging and doubting voices in your head. Remember, we aren't trying to change you, we are trying to resurrect your true spirit. Purpose is not panacea, it is peace, your automated and unconscious mantra to transcend thought.

Use your imagination.

You will need to know your Genetype, accept it, love it, and be true to it to find your purpose. When you consider how many activities and occupations there are in the world, it would be an impossible task for me to give you an exhaustive list, so I have only made broad suggestions. Something I've learned from working with many people on this compels me to repeat that: IT WOULD BE AN IMPOSSIBLE TASK FOR ME TO GIVE YOU AN EXHAUSTIVE LIST, SO I HAVE ONLY MADE BROAD

SUGGESTIONS. *Imagine* all the possibilities, try some on for size, and see how they make you *feel.* I've also given you alternative and imaginative purposes for your Genetype. The breakout section that follows is designed to inspire you to take the brainstorm further, not to be restricted to the short list it offers.

One step back, two steps forward.

Don't be put off fulfilling your purpose because it would mean too much disruption to your life. When the goal you're pursuing is your true purpose in life, it's not a grind, it's bliss, and your motivation to attain it becomes automatic. Sometimes the goal we're frantically channeling our life into is not our purpose, but we are so blinkered and focused on the finish line we don't stop to ask if this is a race we should be running in. As you discover your purpose in life, you may find it clashes with your current predicament or even your ability to pay the bills. But where there is a will, there is a way around any catch-22, and tapping into your true self gives you unlimited will on autopilot. Sometimes you have to take one step back to take two steps forward. You must not let your current life dictate your future life when that future life is your destiny. Your true self, that plant under the rubble, will find a way to express itself whether you like it or not, torturing your existence in surreptitious and sometimes destructive ways until you acknowledge it. You can run from your Genetype, but you can't hide.

Look under your nose.

Don't rule out what you're doing currently as being your purpose. It's possible, perhaps even likely for some Genetypes, that you are already doing what you should be doing each day, only now the voices of doubt in the corridor will cease, the grass will no longer look greener on the other side, and you will now engage your purpose with clarity and renewed verve. You will be at peace, and the wondering about your meaning will end. But be sure you aren't fooling yourself or settling for the sake of laziness or convenience!

Work with the hand you're dealt, not the one you want.

Your true self is who you are, and it's time to make peace with yourself, accepting the Genetypal hand you've been dealt instead of resisting it. Your ego could now try to make you switch Genetypes to suit a loftier purpose, but cheating purpose will ultimately come back to bite you, and your life will be one long Groundhog Day of frustration, something I learned the hard way after an eclectic lifetime of overachievement.

Don't rule out the humble.

Your purpose is not necessarily grand or glamorous; it's often the contrary. Only television and celebrity magazines imply otherwise. You don't need to be an icon to make a difference to the world, you merely have to dig out your soul and take your rightful place in The Global Tribe, and this simple act will have done more for humanity than any Hollywood icon could ever imagine, not to mention achieving a level of immortality that icons would (and do) die for.

Don't make it all about money.

Time is not money; time is *meaning*. While not precluding any purpose, deciding on a purpose or a variation of it purely for money will be a mistake. Treat the money your purpose attracts as a bonus.

It must make time stand still.

I've spoken about "transcending thought" and how you don't watch the clock when time stands still. At such a time you are present, the mind is still, with no care for past or future, and a "hidden hand" is in control. Recall the times in your life you felt this bliss state: a rainy afternoon "wasted" in bed with a true love as you lost track of time, the flavor of your favorite dish singing through your nasal cavity, the rush of adrenaline during a brush with death on a roller coaster. *Feel it.* The core mission of this book is to bring you to this place, permanently and automatically, through finding and living your purpose—a state of bliss that represents your true self. Only three things can grant you this without much conscious effort on your part: food, sex, and death. Though we can imagine giving it a good shot, we can't eat and make love all the time, and suicide is a trifle extreme as a solution, so outside that bliss-trifecta, only having *your purpose as a core value* can take you to your bliss as a constant and automatic state. If what you decide as your purpose doesn't make you feel *at peace*, then you chose unwisely and must start over.

Look under the hood.

It's vital that you become deeply intimate with your Genetype to find your purpose. Don't succumb to the obvious, the literal, and instead get to the *core essence* of your Genetype. People sharing the same Genetype aren't necessarily going to have the same purpose; most of the Genetypes have a *range* of purposes to choose from for the best fit. In the breakout session that follows, I attempt to give you a suggested Genetypal purpose *range*, but you may need to use your imagination for more choices. The *type* of industry you're in isn't as important as what you're doing *within* it, facilitating not such a dramatic change in your life. But don't settle for a false purpose or a compromise for the sake of ease or money. There's going to be an element of trying on the shoes to see if they fit, or at least digging deep into all the everyday elements of any purpose, and then imagining doing it, comparing your life experiences to it, knowing what has given you the most bliss in your past.

Hobbies and interests may or may not be a clue.

Enjoying sex does not make one's purpose a prostitute. Know the difference between pleasure and joy, and what we are searching for is *joy*. But you could get introspective about sex as one example of something that gives you *pleasure*, and ask yourself *what* you enjoy most about it or even *why* you enjoy it. What one person sees purely as a physiological need of life, another person sees as a channel to God. You like playing video games? Hard to imagine this is your purpose in life, but ask yourself what you like about them and what types of games, though I can think of better starting points. The joy of creating something is in all of us, but enjoying writing or painting as a hobby (pleasure) is completely different to being *possessed* with the fundamental *need* to create and compulsively sacrificing sleep/relationships/sanity over creative projects as certain Genetypes do.

Pay attention to the clues of your past.

Cast your mind back and pay attention to *recurring* feelings or signs or moments of bliss like those I've described. Sometimes so many nurture-overlays bury a true self that it moves you in mysterious ways. Recall the moments of bliss outside those of food, sex, and "death," and focus on the times when you felt *compelled* to do something, almost as in a supernatural force possessed you to take action on an ongoing basis, inconsequential of any material reward, and that action soothed your soul. Vice versa for the moments that gave you the *opposite* feeling.

Genetypes aside . . .

Nothing is off the table to you as long as it truly fits your purpose, even if it falls outside the obvious scope of your Genetype. Again, NOTHING IS OFF THE TABLE TO YOU AS LONG AS IT *TRULY* FITS YOUR PURPOSE. It could be an abstract part of your Genetype that gets satisfied, or sometimes a God-given gift shines out regardless and transcends Genetypes and all overlays. Writing, teaching, running your own business, and getting involved in politics could all become channels of purpose that potentially change the world, so these areas have a broad fit as long as *what* you're doing within them is ticking your box of meaning. Remember, the main goal of this book is to bring you happiness through purpose. I only offered Genetypes as a commonly effective pathway to getting it, so don't deny yourself anything as a result of being too much a slave to your Genetype *as long as your true self is driving, not your ego with its wishful thinking.* To repeat something I said in Part One, "You *can* accomplish anything, but there's only one thing you *should.*"

Never say never.

Clarity sparks confidence, and what you have now is clarity, thanks to knowing your Genetype. You must *not* shy away from your purpose if it seems like too lofty a dream! You don't *have* to be world champion of your field of purpose, you just have to *engage* your true self in the activity and drift in the river of joy it takes you to.

Now we will break out into Genetypes. If you come across something that opens your eyes wide and touches you deep down, *pay attention.* Let the raw spirit of your Genetype guide you. You'll know it when your *true self* finds it. Choose wisely . . .

FG-1

Compassion is your Dominant Driver. You have the luxury of being one of the few Genetypes that has your purpose displayed in flashing lights, even if it's an especially bittersweet one: your bliss state is when you're caring for others, especially wounded souls. You will sacrifice for your children or those in your care, no matter what the cost because *it's what you do*. You're proud of this trait, you make no apology for it, and you're baffled why everyone else isn't the same way. But when it comes to choosing exactly what you do each day and how you do it, there are some pitfalls to avoid.

You must choose an activity that actually gets you on the *front lines* of caring for people. For example, working for a charitable organization may sound good, but not so much if you're shuffling paper in the back office. You need to see the person/people in need firsthand and deliver your compassion to them directly. It's also important that your work is mostly focused on that core activity, not just sometimes. Additionally, some activities can *appear* as catering to your purpose, but in practice do not, so be sure to commit to things with both eyes open, especially for someone who doesn't like to disappoint others, as in leaving a job where you're *needed*.

You need to be needed, but nobody needs you like The Global Tribe does right now because compassion has become a scarce resource and is the key to restoring balance in society. With this in mind, consider where you can do the most good, where you can heal the most amount of people. Better still, consider how you can activate compassion in others by giving your gift to a wide audience.

Your purpose spectrum may *appear* limited until you consider your core meaning of simply caring for people in any form.

Occupations such as nurse, nanny, physical therapist, and mother would tick all your obvious boxes. The less obvious could be an emergency room doctor. But compassion can be delivered in many ways to many different people, and you want to witness the effect of your gift on the faces of those you care for. A kindergarten teacher might suit you, especially if you don't have children or they've left the nest, but how would you feel if one of those children wasn't having a happy childhood and there wasn't much you could do about her home life? Working on the front lines of charities that deliver urgent relief supplies could suit you—*seeing* starving children eat. If you thought big, could you start your *own* charity? Would working in hospitality in a Western hotel accomplish something in comparison? Only you can answer this. Don't rule out writing or speaking or counseling, taking your message as far as possible. Starting a business such as a retirement home might also offer you an entrepreneurial angle with total control over care given. A natural-health business might also be a fit if you had access to the results with customers.

Think about how you'll be able to stay in your bliss state until the end. How could you continue to deliver care and compassion when you become elderly and run out of patients/young children?

Think about how to deliver your gift to The Global Tribe in the biggest way possible. Does the extent of your sacrifice to others mean a partial sacrifice of your purpose in order to enter politics or drastically change the structure of a charitable force by sitting in an office?

FG-2

Victory is your Dominant Driver. Your bliss state is to compete/ fight/prove, particularly in typically male-dominated arenas and as part of a team. Provided those boxes are ticked, the spectrum of purpose is wide open for you. You want to stand shoulder to shoulder with men in "battle" (literally or figuratively) and not be seen as any different to them—ideally *better* than them. Your meaning should be obvious to you now, but what you do about it and how is more of a question than others face, and this doesn't frighten you. Most other people yearn to escape the fight, but for you it's the opposite because life is an eternal arena/battleground.

Let's start with a couple of traps you must not fall into. If striving for victory in battle is what you were built for, remember the sayings "Choose your battles" and "Be careful what you wish for." Your ancient programming for competition makes you a potential victim of Beat-the-Jones's Syndrome, your archaic remnants in a modern world deceiving you into perceiving square footage and "stuff" as winning because that's what society has told us means winning, but that is one battle you can't win. Your need for continual competition makes it important to not be stuck in a dead-end job; you need to progress at least until you've reached the top.

You might be particularly attracted to pioneering new ground for female accomplishment; think Amelia Earhart, Hua Mulan, and other FG-2 Genetypes that were here before you.

A Genetype such as yours becomes particularly interesting when we remember the golden rule of "any purpose is suitable as long as it takes you to your personal bliss." You could accomplish this in anything from joining the military to being an airline pilot to running your own business, anything that is male-dominated and allows you to compete/fight/prove and better them. Sports offer a direct outlet for you to compete, whether professionally or otherwise, especially in sports that are male dominated. Your wide range of options means you will have to work harder than most to find the right expression of purpose for you, but you love a challenge, so game on. Your gift can be given to The Global Tribe in so many ways, and the one you may intend least or be conscious of is showing the world that females are and should be considered equal to males. Adding your female intuition to a male-dominated team gives them a sensual edge they previously lacked.

Special note: If you have suffered negative paternal issues in your past—no biological father, a family rift, or abuse—this especially heavy weight for your Genetype can blind you to your purpose and leave you a "wounded warrior," but understand that what happened then does not define you now; your ancient Genetypal clones do.

Think about how you'll be able to stay in your bliss state until the end. How will you compete in a *physical* way when you are elderly? Don't say wheelchair races with men in the care home. Will you need to consider the victory of pen over sword?

Think about how to deliver your gift to The Global Tribe in the biggest way possible. Politics is perfect for this; talk about competitive. Police detective and surgeon are both professions that actually save lives as well as offering you new challenges. And don't forget the title of "First woman to…"

FG-3

Spirituality, connection with The Energy Field is your Dominant Driver. Deep down you know we are from a different time and place, and you are more sensitive to this fact than others who remain unconscious of it. Your meaning is to embrace what you already sense to be true, that a natural energy exists, and that we must stay connected to it, not lose our way. You are a critical force in restoring balance to The Global Tribe, and you must not shy away from your true destiny. *Use* your connection to The Energy Field, tap into it, and let its message flow through your body and into your fingers and/or mouth so you can translate it to the world.

Your perpetual need for isolation serves a purpose in that it allows you valuable time to connect with the spiritual and recharge, but isolation serves no purpose when it is to escape the disturbance in The Energy Field that becomes so apparent to you when among more crowded areas and other (stressed) people. You've been given this power, like it or not; you simply need to embrace it. This is both the gift and the curse of shaman: access to dimensions that others struggle to access.

The Energy Field is trying to communicate with The Global Tribe, and you are its interpreter. Without understanding this, by succumbing to the easy path of simply running away from the disturbances in energy from this lost society, you will gravitate toward activities that offer simplicity but only *appear* to tick your boxes, such as pet breeder or farmer or wildlife reserve warden or even a nun. Those activities may bring you mild happiness or help you avoid the sadness of society, but this is not your full potential or deep bliss state. Writer, spiritual leader, and yoga teacher may be more your purpose and make you the channel between the material and spiritual worlds. Facing crowds is possibly intimidating for you, but the impact you could have on them would be worth it and would make you overcome the fear *when you can witness your impact on negative energy, converting it into positive.* Let The Energy flow *through* you. Don't hold onto it, because that is how the negative can remain with you.

Think about how you'll be able to stay in your bliss state until the end. The Energy Field runs through you until the end and beyond, so have no further thought on this.

Think about how to deliver your gift to The Global Tribe in the biggest way possible. You are shaman, priestess. Along with MG-3, the continual reproduction of your Genetype is what's responsible for the myths, religions, and metaphors repeating in different ways in different cultures around the world, whether you're conscious of it or not, and the deep and life-changing lessons they carry is encoded in your work. I know you didn't ask for this gig, but you are a bridge between past and present, you are a channel between material and spiritual. Learn the myths and one basic religion of our most ancient ancestors, subliminally translate it into the modern tongue with the "hidden hand" as your guide, find and inspire FG-3s and MG-3s who will outlive you, and pass on the message of our lengthy past. Come out of hiding. This is your code, your craft, and your calling.

FG-4

Creative expression is your Dominant Driver, perhaps to your surprise. There is a great deal more to you than you and others may see at surface level. Underneath the symbol of femininity is where your true meaning hides: creative expression, and not simply because you're a born actress. What people don't understand is that, much like MG-3, you're a born creative artist only, unlike MG-3, your creative work isn't necessarily a separate entity to you; *you* are the work. Your face and body are the canvas you paint on, and the many different paths into a creative world are your true meaning. You aren't necessarily a classically beautiful woman, but you have sex appeal with the way you carry yourself and the alluring clothes you wear (often starting fashion trends by yourself)—look closely and objectively at Marilyn Monroe and you'll see this.

Your purpose is also to bring out The Goddess in other women, directly or by example, and when you do so, your perceived threat is replaced by what you stand for. "This is what raw femininity looks like."

The really obvious purposes you may consider are, as suspected, actress, singer, dancer, model, etc. But also, if you want a less competitive field that additionally focuses on bringing out The Goddess in others and more control over creativity, consider less obvious activities such as fashion designer, makeup artist, costume designer, and beautician. In ancient times, I can picture you placing flower necklaces on females, but let's now consider your deeper purpose and how you can deliver your gift to The Global Tribe in other ways.

Think about how you'll be able to stay in your bliss state until the end. Find a purpose that ideally blends your joy of spotlight with creativity but also that has longevity, to include a pathway for later life and growing old gracefully without attaching your happiness completely to appearances. For example, being a model usually has an expiration date, but if this leads to photography or fashion design, then good. Being an actress is something you can take into later life, or perhaps transitioning to off-camera talent instead.

Think about how to deliver your gift to The Global Tribe in the biggest way possible. You have the potential purpose of creating an invention that improves lives (conception stage only, so partner with another Genetype for the rest), being a life coach, or writing/painting/photography to make people think and to make people *love*. You aren't meant to be understood, even by yourself, because love is not meant to be understood. You're sometimes accused of being superficial, that with you it's all on the surface. They're right, but not in the way they think, for your true purpose lies deep within you, waiting to be activated. You represent something sacred, something lost and waiting to be found. Show us your true meaning.

FG-5

Protecting the vulnerable is your Dominant Driver. You must fight for a cause, compete, and above all else, *protect*. "Feminist" is really only a contemporary label society may give your Genetype, but what's *truly* woven into your genes is your inherent desire to fight for the independence and equality of others, particularly the vulnerable. Notice how common it is to see your Genetype also identifying with the fight for causes like gay rights, transgender recognition, and racial equality, so "feminist" is really too limiting a term for you and your formidable abilities.

You are the predominant counterforce to patriarchy, and you (rightly) even consider the planet as something vulnerable that needs protection from exploitation, a cause that has nothing to do with feminism. I promised I would not make ancient comparisons, but your Genetype is the hardest to resist and is portrayed throughout human mythology as wielding a bow and arrows (a weapon that's been dated to over 60,000 years ago). As guardian of the vulnerable element of a tribe, skill with a bow would've allowed you to pick off multiple targets from a distance before they could get to those you protect. Hence, your Genetype often possesses good hand-eye coordination.

As long as you're loyal to your Dominant Driver, there is a range of options open to your purpose, and a decision to make between pen and sword about how you enter this role. You *need* to stand on a wall between the vulnerable and those who would oppress them. You want to make a difference, ideally in the prevention of attack against the vulnerable, but failing that, in working with the victims and discouraging further violations. Revolving around your Dominant Driver opens a surprisingly wide purpose spectrum, and you'll now understand why certain Genetypes feel torn between ludicrously different career choices such as journalist or police officer!

Activities that would fall under "pen" might be journalist, editor, human resources professional, lawyer (criminal, civil rights), politician, and charitable worker for causes that involve protecting women and children. Activities that would fall under "sword" could be police officer, soldier (in a defensive role, not offensive), firefighter, medic, social services worker (child abuse, domestic violence, rape), self-defense instructor, women's shelter volunteer. Your formidable force opens you up to business applications and business ownership but could potentially compromise your purest form of purpose.

Think about how you'll be able to stay in your bliss state until the end. As you age, the "sword" options will become less available, so you must transition to "pen" at that point, if not before. Experience in journalism or publishing may lead you to write or own a publishing business or consult. Stay influential.

Think about how to deliver your gift to The Global Tribe in the biggest way possible. Politics is a path you can take into your senior years that allows you a platform to fight for matriarchy at the highest levels of influence, for you don't need to be on the front lines; you simply require results. *So pick up your arrows and clear the path for The Matriarch's return to prominence*, to restore the balance between The Masculine and The Feminine. She's counting on you. We all are, even though most people don't know it or appreciate it.

FG-6

Healing is your Dominant Driver, but you probably never even suspected as much at a conscious level, and I strongly doubt you are living this purpose already. An awakening for you is perhaps the most surprising and dramatic of all the Genetypes. Pre-awakening, your purpose seems to be simply having freedom and fun with a safety net. Post-awakening, once you lose your rose-tinted glasses on life, you transform into a guide for others, a healer, and some-one people can go to for help. In this dramatic transformation, your innocence is traded in for leadership and bravery.

In your initial Genetype description, I referenced Ridley Scott's film *Thelma and Louise*, with you as *Thelma*. *Thelma* starts the story as a flighty, irresponsible girl who has an uncanny talent for attracting trouble that (FG-5 protector) *Louise* keeps rescuing her from, climaxing in *Louise* executing a man *after* he tried to rape *Thelma*, sending them both on the run from the law. Notice how by the end of *Thelma and Louise's* journey, *Thelma* becomes the braver of the pair, even leading *Louise*, and finally driving off a cliff rather than being captured by the agents of patriarchy, the latter being *her* idea, not fearless *Louise's*. *Dorothy* eventually exposed *The Wizard of Oz* and then stuck it to him with both barrels for the deception, forcing him to heal her companions, one way or another. *Dorothy's* and *Thelma's* journeys are modern-myth illus-trations of your purpose of taking your place as guide and healer.

If I was pandering to the pre-awakening version of you, I would point to careers such as event planner, tour guide, cruise ship entertainer, or perhaps public relations professional. Pre-awakening, you are built for playtime, so play. If you really must work, then choose an activity with perpetually changing action and scenery, something that gets you attention and into society, something fun, and ideally with flexible hours.

Post-awakening must be where you are headed for true purpose, though, and you take the good qualities of children with you in an awakening: empathy, innocence, and curiosity. But now you are drawn more to healing others, listening to them, and tuning into their needs because you have now crossed the river of fire that they face. The question is: how can you meet your destiny and cross that necessary river of fire you need to awaken? *Thelma* had a continuous brush with danger and death, but what will you do? As a catalyst for awakening, consider ways of transitioning between the pre-awakened and post-awakened purposes, perhaps by combining social events with therapy. For example, dating clubs for niche markets such as disabled or trauma victims. You don't necessarily have to experience danger for yourself, you only need exposure to the effects of it.

Think about how you'll be able to stay in your bliss state until the end. Writing, teaching, counseling, and speaking will allow you an eternal platform to guide and heal.

Think about how to deliver your gift to The Global Tribe in the biggest way possible. Ultimately you must be headed for occupations such as therapist, counselor, and psychologist, and delivering your message by writing or speaking or doing charitable work will make as many people whole again as possible, bravely leading wounded souls out of darkness and into the light of hope, to rejoin our Global Tribe.

FG-7

Partnering is your Dominant Driver. On the surface, it's very simple: to find and marry The One, and then to be the best partner you can be to them, together *as equals* until death do you part. The interesting part of your Genetype is that it overlaps with the next part of the book on love, because you're the only Genetype whose purpose is intertwined with your romantic relationship with one person. Where it goes wrong is if your partner misreads your idolizing of them as weakness and takes advantage of it, elevating himself or herself above you (typically if that partner is male).

That's why you make their life hell when they attempt this, usually by temporarily abandoning them. This potential disharmony is symbolic of the male-female dynamic in the patriarchal society of today.

Your purpose should have always been obvious, but your motive is often misunderstood by both supporters of patriarchy and matriarchy alike—the former disrespecting you and taking advantage of you, the latter misreading you as everything they're fighting against, and both of them plain wrong because you represent *balance*. Matriarchy isn't about females ruling; it's about females being equal, side by side with males. Assuming matriarchy is about females being on top is the result of a mere few thousand years of patriarchal thinking. Our ancient past explains how males and females are equal, if anything females being slightly above men, and I will talk more about this as the book unfolds. The inherent love and kindness of The Feminine makes your side of this equation appear weak to the wrong type of (usually male) partner.

So the hard part for you is perhaps finding the right partner or not being with the right partner, and being comfortable in your bliss despite contemporary society's attempts to ridicule and demean it. Additionally, you *must* have an alternative plan that meets your needs to be a matriarch in the event you lose your partner or never find them. Remember, if you chose the wrong partner, especially a man who is not fit to be your "king," you must not be afraid to leave and start over, because partnering is your purpose in life. What makes the right partner? You need someone who is a strong leader type but who can remain balanced and at your side as an equal. If you have no other choice but to work, ensure it fits the matriarchal role by having a surrogate "family" to watch over and support.

Think about how you'll be able to stay in your bliss state until the end. You may well outlive your partner, but that is a reality you face bravely, idolizing their spirit when they've departed.

Think about how to deliver your gift to The Global Tribe in the biggest way possible. There *is* life outside your partner's happiness and your family, and you could find a way to spread your meaning and show your natural leadership. You represent The Matriarch, and you must doggedly continue to dig your heels in for partners as equals, never suffering subjugation.

MG-1

Logic is your Dominant Driver, and what a broad range of disciplines this entails: communication, cooperation, analysis, motivation, organization, systems technology, to name a few. Underneath it all is a need to bring order from chaos, to engender and oversee cooperation. You must be among others, working with them, uniting them, forging a path to a common goal for the greater good, and the result is all the reward you need. You need to feel useful in a structured and civilized society. Your ancient past translates well into the present-day corporate or governmental "tribes," and you're the glue of today's workforces.

You're one of the more blessed Genetypes when it comes to finding your purpose because you have such choice, and because chances are your current career likely gives you purpose, as it's a good fit for modern society, only now you can enjoy the lucidity of knowing that you're doing what you're supposed to. You're a career animal, so the main thing is to be part of a team in a large organization or to be an independent contractor who can be made to feel like part of that team with your clients. You need to be on the go, planning, and moving toward goals. Hacking your way to starting your own large business isn't going to be as suitable, so try not to get sucked into that trap, perhaps out of a need for more order; better to change to a more structured and orderly organization and play to your strengths of logic and teamwork. If an employer doesn't recognize you as the gift you are, then move on or consult.

The more obvious type of careers would be accountant, scientist, manager, engineer, consultant, programmer, etc. But there are other doors open to you that you may have never let your imagination run to that still tick all your boxes: airline pilot, IRS agent, detective, military intelligence officer, judge/attorney, doctor/surgeon, financial analyst. My list of purposes could never be exhaustive for you, but you're the type of person who is more inclined to require one, so here's an idea to spark your imagination. This book covers a wide range of topics. As you read through, pay attention to which topics raise an eyebrow and see where this thought takes you, as long as you're being true to your core needs for purpose: using logic and working as part of a team.

Think about how you'll be able to stay in your bliss state until the end. Retirement and redundancies are a reality of a rapidly changing world, and both threaten to destroy your bliss state, even causing you severe health problems from the trauma of them. The trick will be to remember your Dominant Driver and understand that career isn't your purpose; using your teamwork skills is. This is something you can take into your later years, such as HOA management, charity management, etc. But you *must* continue to work, for the sake of yourself and others.

Think about how to deliver your gift to The Global Tribe in the biggest way possible. Great challenges lay ahead of humanity, and your talent for negotiation talks could be instrumental, as could a scientific breakthrough. Also, you could influence corporations toward more environmentally responsible policies and play a part in staving off human extinction.

MG-2

Knowledge is your Dominant Driver. The simplicity of being able to contemplate the complex is all you require—to explore life's inner meaning, to accumulate ideas and develop theories, and *to relay them*. Note my emphasis on "relay them." You're too intelligent with too much to contribute to keep your ideas to yourself. To reach your bliss state you must go beyond the acquisition and distillation of knowledge; you must deliver the fruits of it to the world and be recognized for doing so.

You need to be left alone with your thoughts and have the freedom to express the ideas that emerge as a result. The expression of your ideas could be the challenging part, but also essential, for you gain the satisfaction of seeing a possible impact on the world, and the Internet can assist you without having to leave the house. Start exploring mediums to get your ideas out there and even providing you an income. Public speaking in some form would also be a powerful medium that has the healthy side effect of completing you by forcing you to become more social and sympathetic to the people you're philosophizing about, as well as adding a more practical line of research to your theses if you enveloped the attendees as a focus group.

With these bliss requirements in mind, avoid paths that may have seemed right to you before and are even *similar* to your correct path but don't tick your boxes quite enough. For example, high school teacher could sound tempting, but college professor gives you more of that intellectual freedom you need. The artistic side of you could appreciate art as a form of philosophy, and you would make an astute critic.

What it's really about for you is the *need to know and understand.* Scientist, inventor, engineer, author, media specialist, and psychologist dive into this basic need. Once you've got that base covered, it's a matter of deciding the outlet you'll relay your ideas through because you must not let it all simply bounce around and decay in your head! Being a monk would fit your purpose in many ways, but not completely because there's a part of you deep down that wants to change the world.

Think about how you'll be able to stay in your bliss state until the end. You're one of the fortunate Genetypes who can usually have no restrictions to purpose caused by old age, and your mind will stay active as well as enjoying the benefit of years of knowledge.

Think about how to deliver your gift to The Global Tribe in the biggest way possible. You see an alien world and want to be a force for changing it at a systemic level, *so what's stopping you?* It's tempting for you to lock yourself away, despairing at the daunting task of changing the trajectory of a lost society, but now you know there are many more Genetypes like you around the world, and, activated together, you will be a force for change. So it all begins with that intelligent man in the mirror.

MG-3

Creative expression is your Dominant Driver. Pen, paintbrush, guitar, camera, pan, or chisel, *pick it up and tell a story.* You have the gift of *vision* and can see what could become of a cold block of marble or a vacant piece of land. During moments of pure inspiration (and anger) it's as if someone or something is using you as a vessel to communicate through, like your actions are working faster than your head. That's The Energy Field talking to the world through you. Embracing that and its ambassador,

The Muse, letting her energy flow through you *on her schedule* and articulating what she's saying, is your meaning. You are her microphone, like it or not. Many people who don't possess the gift of your Genetype aspire to be you, so be grateful and do what you were put here to do. If you master your disposition, channel your gift creatively, and populate your vivid imagination with cathedrals instead of concentration camps, you could be an inspiration to humanity, your work admired and analyzed for centuries after your time. Better still, your work could make people *happy* and bring hope and joy to where there is none.

As long as you are engaged in creative expression, letting pure inspiration possess you, you are in your bliss state and have transcended more than most Genetypes, once you are there. Once this need is met, you are living out your purpose, and it's only a question of how you'll express yourself. The obvious choices for you dictate the channel of expression: writer, director, songwriter, photographer, chef, painter, sculptor, and designer. But make it count because you are here to shake the ground, to disrupt the status quo with your storms, to introduce a little chaos, and balance our inclination toward idle conformity.

Alternative roles, usually in more commercial and more reliably lucrative areas, will compromise your purpose to a degree, depending on how restricted your expression is in order to cater to market forces. You may have inadvertently wandered into one of these alternative roles, not previously knowing your Genetype: advertiser (creative team only), architect, property developer (doing this correctly requires vision—a fixer-upper or piece of vacant land becomes your canvas), computer games creator (ideas, not technical), or inventor (concept only). Notice how your purpose becomes lost if you get involved in the execution of an idea as opposed to its birth.

Think about how you'll be able to stay in your bliss state until the end. The Muse will whisper in your ear until your last breath, so have no fear on this one.

Think about how to deliver your gift to The Global Tribe in the biggest way possible. You are shaman—the priests of our ancient past. Along with FG-3, the continual reproduction of your Genetype is what's responsible for the myths, religions, and metaphors repeating in different ways in different cultures around the world, whether you're conscious of it or not, and the deep and life-changing lessons they carry is encoded in your work. I know you didn't ask for this gig, but you are a bridge between past and present, you are a channel between material and spiritual. Learn the myths and one basic religion of our most ancient ancestors, subliminally translate it into the modern tongue with The Muse as your guide, find and inspire FG-3s and MG-3s who will outlive you, and pass on the message of our long past. This is your code, your craft, and your calling.

MG-4

Philosophy is your Dominant Driver; this is the cause, and obsession with women is merely the symptom. Pop the hood and consider what's behind your obsession with women. Much like Female Genetype 6, there is an "awakening" element implicit to your Genetype, assuming you'd like to enjoy the considerable benefits of committing to only one partner.

It would be easy for me to dismiss the meaning of life for you as simply being "women," and offer a list of purpose ideas that would suit, but there's something at the heart that also needs considering: *an unconscious search for a maternal figure*, a quest for the perfect woman, for The Sacred Feminine. Our ancient genes quietly crave the goddess worship that was imprinted on human DNA for the vast majority of our existence, but yours more than most. When you consider that philosophy is the study of the fundamental nature of existence, you can begin to understand that you are a temporally displaced disciple of The Goddess. It's about intrigue, not conquest. This seed of knowledge might inspire you for further introspection and spur your (possibly latent) interest in the esoteric, art, or philosophy, opening new doorways of purpose such as teaching or writing. The reason life-goal completion has evaded you thus far is lack of motivation, and that's because nothing has excited you enough yet (apart from women!) because you've been unaware of your true meaning. Now that has changed.

How to define your gift to The Global Tribe, then? It must surely be to restore The Feminine to former glory, to figuratively paint her on temple ceilings. People who thought you a womanizer misunderstand how important your awakened state is. We could list activities such as female companionship services, hairstylist, barman, or strip club owner, and they would tick all your boxes at a superficial level, giving you happiness but not your bliss state. You love women, you hate work, and you love to party. That wish list sounds more like pleasure than joy, and there is more to you than that.

Think about how you'll be able to stay in your bliss state until the end. This is what will encourage you to get to the heart of your disposition; your options for women chasing shall narrow to a depressing degree when you are elderly. And that is the time when you shall also regret not committing to one woman who, now you can see all female Genetypes, will not be perfect. Your quest to find the perfect woman has been a metaphorical one; you just didn't know it until now.

Think about how to deliver your gift to The Global Tribe in the biggest way possible. You are here to show us how to embrace the wild and unpredictable side of our nature, not repress it, which is why you're often perceived as an outcast. But that goes with the territory, so stay true to your meaning no matter how many stones society throws at you. You might consider a career in any of the arts, particularly acting. Make the world see what you now see: The quest for the perfect woman is an unconscious quest for a return to The Divine, a quest to find what has been lost. Teach, write, speak, shout, and love women *as a group*, making reservations in your heart for just *one* special woman, forever, who is not perfect, but who is perfect for *you*.

MG-5

Freedom is your Dominant Driver. Your meaning is as simple as your needs are: to feel alive, never standing still, with the wind in your hair, letting a never-ending story be told instead of being the one to tell it. You are a "merry wanderer of the night," like Puck in *A Midsummer Night's Dream*, a playful adventurer like Peter Pan. You will never feel any shame for your nature, and it will never change; it is your very meaning. At the heart of your nature is identification with the innocence of children, thus the unwavering defense of your nature that makes you resistant to change or growing up—because children have more fun. Who's to say that this isn't the correct way to live? Society does, and you should now know what society is.

How can you commit to only one purpose when you perpetually need to fly away and be free? There appear to be two obvious options: 1) Suck it up and make as much money as possible to create a passive income that would allow you to play all day. 2) Find work that either encompasses freedom and variety or that speaks to your core meaning, such as working with children or having a playful role such as those in the entertainment industry. Vocations that require a constant variety of hours, location, and "duties" would also work well, such as acting—a justifiable way to live multiple characters, embrace fantasies, and let loose.

Work that meets your core needs varies from flying instructor to fisherman. The wind must be in your sails, you have a compulsion for adventure, and you must embrace this need, not suppress it, however much contrary pressure you feel from society. You have no need for trappings and "stuff," so you could retire at a young age on a lot less than most people "need," making freedom to simply play all day closer than you might think, and living in a mobile camper would keep your scenery changing. With your Genetype, the critical point isn't so much about what to make your purpose as what to ensure it's *not*. Think back to the "nightmares" listed when you first discovered your Genetype. Getting tied down and corporate drudgery will kill your soul.

Think about how you'll be able to stay in your bliss state until the end. Part of your inner journey must be to see that freedom doesn't have to exist purely in the material plane but also in the spiritual, the freedom from ego. Growing old means facing the reality of growing up because whatever you think, the mirror will contradict you more and more with age. You must learn to not fear death and to appreciate that your consciousness, your Genetype, will live on.

Think about how to deliver your gift to The Global Tribe in the biggest way possible. When you live according to purpose, you give your gift by encouraging people to be light of heart. Deep down, you are an entertainer, you make us smile as a child would, and you give us the medicine of laughter. When we take life too seriously, we become brittle, and brittle things snap easily. Look around at the world today and we see a dangerous amount of snapping. A child is a symbol of our true self. As resolute as Peter Pan, stay true to yourself, bring home the "lost boys" and girls of today's society, and bring "Mr. Darling" home to his children. Bring us *all* home.

MG-6

Protecting, perhaps even battle itself, is your Dominant Driver. Any student of history would have difficulty denying that man apparently has a grim *need* for battle, and you are a symbol of this need. You struggle to understand why nobody sees this, dancing around the issues with words, and you want them to feel as you do. You are the male counterpart of Female Genetype 4; where she is an ancient symbol of unchecked femininity, you are an ancient symbol of unchecked masculinity.

Selecting your purpose is simple for a simple guy: you must get physical. Most little boys grow up playing at the sort of things you're best suited to do, but you must actually *do* them as an adult. The corporate world will kill your spirit, so stay away. You've little interest in retirement plans, salaries, and business cards.

The obvious vocations for you will come as no surprise, and they should all be fulfilling for you, but activate your imagination and let out the protector within you in other ways by seriously considering the less obvious, especially if you feel more altruistic or more intellectually inclined. Firefighting, the military, and contact sports are all perfect occupations for you, each giving a great gift to the Global Tribe, and each giving you a bliss state once you're in the heat of the action, so ensure your posting gets you as much front-line activity as possible.

Let's now think out of the box for ways to tick all your boxes and set your imagination in motion. Stuntman and bush pilot would work, but keep thinking. Active protection means getting into the action. The more entrepreneurially minded may consider a security or personal protection agency. Front-line crisis-zone cameraman also gets you in the thick of it and gives protection an additional meaning: depiction of horrific situations to the rest of the world.

Think about how you'll be able to stay in your bliss state until the end. You do not fear death, but becoming elderly and less active is a problem for you. Turning more to the instruction side of things will help: fitness instructor, athletic coach, firearms instructor, etc. Ultimately, your words will be all you have left to protect others, so you must become a *spiritual* warrior, helping others to protect themselves from the greatest threat that exists: themselves.

Think about how to deliver your gift to The Global Tribe in the biggest way possible. The fortunate aspect of purposes such as firefighter is that it saves lives, and saving a life saves the world. But there are even grander ideals that fit your Genetype; think of those boat captains who sail between harpoon and whale. Force may sometimes be required to rescue society from its growing insanity, and you are the man for the job.

MG-7

Power is your Dominant Driver. Your ancient genes are unconsciously searching for a kingdom or tribe to lead, and without one you come unglued. You mean well; even Hitler believed he was doing the right thing by the German people who, until the tide of the war turned, did see their lives improve (provided they weren't Jewish, elderly, infirmed, or displaying non-Aryan features). Your confidence means that you know what a great leader you could be if only people would flock to your banner, so it frustrates you when they don't see that. But respect is earned, not demanded at gunpoint, or you're not a leader; you're a jackbooted thug. Study the greatest leaders of history and what made them great, and you will find your true purpose.

People are desperate to play follow-the-leader, so if it's power and respect you want, then it shouldn't be difficult. But garnering power the wrong way will ultimately cause you to *lose* power. Consider history. We will always need leaders, but we *never* need dictators. You have to choose which kind of "ruler" to be: a Roman Emperor or a 1930s dictator. The Roman Empire lasted for hundreds of years because the idea of Rome was bigger than any one emperor, and it made life *better* for the countries it conquered (integrating those peoples to such a degree that Christianity was eventually able to effectively take it over without destroying it). Hitler didn't enjoy the same length of reign at little over ten years, and notice how he took his own life to avoid admitting he was wrong. Of course, you'd never do something like that . . .

Finding your happiness is simple: gaining total obedience and respect from "subjects." You will drink yourself to death before forced to live as the "inferior" subjects you attempt to rule over. Any other Genetypes who might be reading this probably think I'm being flippant toward you, but you and I both know you're nodding your head to all I say. Your total lack of duality and self-doubt is what makes you a born leader.

If in the private sector, you're most likely to have your own business or be CEO of a large business, as long as nobody can tell you what to do, because that will make you deeply unhappy. You have an inclination not simply to be happy with having your own business but to have a world-dominating, game-changing business, but this could be your undoing. Work with a strict accountant because your ego and need to be on top could break your company with overspending or overextending itself.

Failing attaining high ranks in politics or business, choose something in government that puts you behind a badge and grants you absolute power in a certain field and ideally behooves people to kiss your ring.

Think about how you'll be able to stay happy until the end. As you retire, look at positions such as president of local organizations and charities or HOAs.

Think about how to deliver your gift to The Global Tribe in the biggest way possible. The day you do is the day you defeat ego and change the world in a way few other Genetypes can. Notice how I've only used the word "happiness" for you so far. *Bliss* is a different state, and only when you slay your mighty ego can you be a *truly* great leader who is remembered and respected long after your death. Set the example to other MG-7s, showing them the *true* power that comes from compassion, balance, and gratitude, because when *you* do this, incredible things can happen.

Moving Mountains

"For God has planted them like strong and graceful oaks for his own glory." Isaiah 61:3

Saving yourself saves the world. Without purpose we are without a compass but still left wanting. In Western society this unfulfilled wanting has nowhere to go but excessive consumerism and over-consumption. Overconsumption = "boom and bust" cycle = economic depressions = trade wars = shooting wars. And: Over-consumption = depletion and pollution of planet = ecological disaster = human extinction. You don't have to be a political activist to save the world, you just have to find your purpose in it.

There is no higher esteem to be found than knowing who you are and being proud of who you are, in other words, when you possess self-confidence that is immune to the exogenous. Your quest entails escaping from The System, and it is a righteous quest, so do not fear shunning from a society that is sleepwalking and that channels its energy into consumerism as a dangerous substitute for individual purpose. Living for "stuff" is not living. If you've chosen your purpose correctly, you should have felt your internal "wanting valve" clank over to a different setting, channeling your wanting energy away from the mindless consumption-consolation complex proliferating society and toward purpose. Don't check any more baggage than you need to on this journey, don't simulate success *a la Joneses.*

When you've succeeded in finding your true purpose, elation may be matched by intimidation, but there is no turning back now you've seen truth. If you chose your purpose correctly, you already know this. If you aren't currently feeling a heady cocktail of anxiety and excitement from your choice, then you did not yet reveal your purpose and you should search more deeply, stripping yourself of any restriction your ego may perceive. The dreams that come true are those forged in the fires of our bellies, and it takes having a purpose-centered dream to ignite the required will that lies dormant within us. We get what we think. Most people think about what they *don't* want, and so that's what they get.

If you're fortunate to have discovered that you're honestly already living your purpose, you now have validation and lucidity to be and remain in your bliss without apology. If not, any intimidation or anxiety you feel may be because the task of living your purpose seems too great a challenge, or you're wondering how to derive an income from it, or perhaps you don't know where to begin or how to find your way back to that true path, or maybe you're worried about the repercussions from people around you or society itself. I know there's much to consider with any life change, bills to pay, kids to raise, but this is your destiny. *Amor Fati* (love fate).

"How can I be of service?" Your true colors shine vibrantly when living a life according to your personal truth, when you aren't living a *lie*. When you enter your bliss state, you feel a sensation of being humbled and hollowed out that can only be described as *love*. And in that moment you feel chosen, you feel love flow through you, and you begin to love *yourself*. Only then can you see a road to a bliss state that can even transcend purpose.

part four

THE
FORK
IN THE
ROAD

Who's Driving?

You now know who you are and why you're here. Only when you know thyself can you love thyself (or how would you know what to love?). And only when you love thyself can you fully give, and hence receive, *true* love. Without love of self you could be stuck in a continuous loop of unhappy relationships as you project your unconscious self-loathing onto others, hence the common retort, "It takes one to know one."

How do our ancient genes guide us through the part of our life map that is the most mystifying and magical? The answer depends on which one of you is navigating—your false self or your true self, and this represents a crucial and continuous fork in the road for your personal relationships, both for existing ones and the new ones you choose. At the end of Part Two, I compared your now severed false self to a child that clings to your side, a needy cluster of insecurities that will always be there, only separate. I will also now refer to your true self and false self as your "higher self" and "lower self," respectively, symbolic of that child being lower than you. Your lower self is no different to other animals in that it acts unconsciously and selfishly, but your higher self represents a consciousness that separates human animals from other animals. The quality of your romantic journey is a direct function of whether your lower or higher self is driving, and they each want to take a different direction at this fork in the relationship road: mindless animal or conscious human being?

What happens if you follow the easier, more seductive path of the mindless animal, the lower self? First, this means other people are dealing with the worst parts of your ego, and so, unsurprisingly, this results in a chain reaction of unhappiness, exacerbated when you're exposed to your partner's lower self. A mindless animal is entirely selfish as part of its primitive programming, so the best your lower self can offer is a selfish and conditional "love" loaded with the potential for insecurity, infidelity, anger, and vengeance. The walls between you and a partner gradually build up until you eventually can't see each other over the wall, and one day you wake up next to a stranger.

Second, letting your lower self choose the fork in the relationship road means you are at the mercy of The Energy Field's prime directive: reproduction for survival of the species and how it's pro-grammed us to find others attractive. Most Internet dating sites and "Swipe for Sex" apps are at least initially based on this level of attraction, severing us from any instincts about a person's energy, making this a "filter" that is highly limited, at best. At this purely superficial level, humans are unconsciously scanning for facial symmetry in a potential partner because this indicates healthy genes. Fair hair on a female suggests higher estrogen levels, meaning higher fertility. Heterosexual males are unconsciously assessing a female's hip-to-waist ratio for the ideal of 10:8 for the purposes of healthy impregnation and birthing, and mammary glands for milk production. Contemporary females make themselves sick to imitate the stick insect celebrities in magazines, but it's not what males really want if they're honest; it's about *ratio*, not size or weight. Heterosexual females are unconsciously assessing for small and muscular buttocks for sexual thrusting and deep insemination, and yes, penis length, for ejaculation as close to the awaiting egg as possible.

Superficial attraction is a healthy and normal thing that The Energy Field has ingeniously and insidiously installed in our hardwiring. It can be a mere component of a loving relationship, it could give birth to a loving relationship, but it is not love. In this sense, The Energy Field's agenda is not necessarily aligned with your personal happiness or even your sexual pleasure. For example, on the popular topic of penis size (or unpopular, depending on one's penis size), heterosexual females who act with their lower selves are genetically programmed to be attracted to longer penises, perhaps even creating a self-fulfilling prophecy, and yet female orgasm induces from two points totally unrelated to penis length. There is no sexual bliss for a female in a large object banging against her cervix, but it creates juicy urban myths and mindless chatter.

So, bruised egos and cervixes await you on the path taken by the lower self. But cynics and scientists may say the fork in the road of the lower self is the only option, arguing that love is a purely functional thing, a social utility genetically programmed into us for mating and nurturing, which is true, but if that's *all* it is, then why do we love people who've died? We can feel love toward a creative artist like a musician or an actor without even meeting that artist, because their work touched our soul. We can love animals. There is no reproductive value in these things, so The Energy Field must have something else in mind, something abstract and hidden for this other fork in the road taken by the higher self. If we can love people who've died or people we've never met, *love transcends space and time.* Perhaps love relates to another dimension we can't readily perceive, a dimension that our ancient ancestors evidently sought to access.

Our Mother

When we consider that human existence began around 2.5 million years ago in the region surrounding Egypt, and that Egyptian pyramids are spiritual centers for an ancient stellar-religion, it stands to reason that Egyptian mythology is our purest link to any basic religion of humanity that would've been imprinted onto our genetic memory at least over the past 70,000 years, at the dawn of The Cognitive Revolution.

What is probably the oldest "fairy tale" is found at the core of Egyptian mythology in the story of the god Osiris and the goddess Isis, and in this story it is the *female* (Isis) who rescues the male (Osiris), not the male rescuing the female, as we are accustomed. The contemporary fairy tale *ends* with a wedding, but in the original fairy tale the wedding has already taken place. Isis's husband, Osiris, is murdered, placed in a casket, and cast onto a river. Isis embarks on a relentless quest to find her husband. Even though he is dead, her true love for him runs so deep. In the "happily ever after," she finds a way to join with him, after all, in a remarkable and symbolic way that I'll come back to later in the book.

The Greeks borrowed Egyptian mythology, and their stories are perhaps more familiar to you. Theseus only defeated The Minotaur because of Princess Ariadne's true love for him, risking her own life to discover how to escape the labyrinth so she could relay the secret to Theseus. (The Minotaur, as most mythological monsters, is a metaphor for ego. "Ariadne" was also the name of the "maze builder" in the recent film *Inception*, where she helped "Cobb" through the dream maze to confront his personal demons.) These are stories where males and females work together as a team, *as equal partners*, not a helpless female hiding behind a male for rescue, contrary to the more recent Grimm Brothers' evolution of the tales. The *true and original* fairy tale is about males and females in equal balance so that they may access the higher dimension reserved for human animals—a higher love through our higher selves, *to become one.*

Today, there is no such ideal. *True* love is the doorway to masculinity devoid of misogyny, but this is a balance that modern males often struggle with, depriving both them and their partner of The Higher Love. Many contemporary males snigger about "sissy love talk," but the same "tough guys" who would do so have also literally cried on my shoulder for lack of love or fear of losing love. Modern society conditions males to provide and protect, to not show emotion, but the fact is that princes need rescuing from dragons as much as princesses—*more so* when you appreciate that the "dragon" is a metaphor for ego.

We now live in a patriarchal world where most women are placed on a spectrum that spans from unconscious discrimination to slavery, where they are seen as weak or inferior to men in some way. Most women think twice before walking down an alleyway or simply past a construction site for fear of harassment or worse, and they can't even sit alone at a bar without most people thinking they're looking for a one-night stand. The tacky stench of furthering oneself for sexual favors still hangs in the air. When a man sleeps around, he's a "player." When a woman sleeps around, she's a "whore." Someone's wife/daughter/mother/sister is treated like an animal. Is this who we are? Is there anything hidden in our ancient genes to explain this superior attitude of males over females?

All embryos are inherently female and only become male in the womb from the addition of hormones, like testosterone. This is why men have nipples, an enlarged clitoris called a "penis," and a visible seam to seal up a scrotum that stops it becoming labia.

There is estrogen in men, and there is testosterone in women, varying in degrees between individuals. Considering the biological process, there is nothing unnatural about humans, regardless of sex, spanning the intricate spectrum of gender preference, sexual preference, and romantic relations. The Higher Love is a union of souls, of spiritual form, not material.

What about the baby argument, the notion that a woman's purpose is merely to give birth to and raise children, whereas the male's purpose is purely to provide for them? When the first humans stood upright on their hind legs, they developed narrower hips, and this caused females to give birth earlier than the animals they previously were; human babies cannot walk from birth, whereas most other newborn animals can. This tied new human mothers to nurturing a newborn, but there is no convincing evidence to say that this tied her to a male to provide for her. Other females could've provided for her, and even if not, she would've had basic foraging skills that required minimal exertion, even when pregnant or with a newborn on her back, such as picking berries and trapping rabbits. Judging by the Genetype profiles, some females even hunted and protected *alongside* males as their primary purpose. So our contemporary perception of females being helpless and dependent on males is an aberration and a function of a mere few thousand years of propaganda, an amount of time that genetic inertia scoffs at.

Don't compare modern humans' relatively softer lifestyle and limited skill set with our ancient ancestors; as a society they may have been less technologically advanced, but as individuals they left us in the dust. Foraging tribes would've moved quickly and stealthily, their senses as tuned to the environment as the other animals they competed with, each tribe member a capable and sturdy individual, including females. If even the toughest contemporary male went back in time 70,000 years and stumbled into the wrong part of the forest, a forager female could have opened his throat with a flint knife before he realized he wasn't alone. And she'd have fashioned that knife from bare rock only a few minutes earlier.

In Part One I explained how Homo sapiens possessing superior *social* skills is the likely reason for their existence as the sole human species, something more genetically gifted to females. With all this in mind, contemporary scientists remain puzzled about why ancient societies appear to have been patriarchal and not matriarchal. Scientists are often shackled to specialized fields that prevent them from seeing the bigger picture. And how far back are they defining as "ancient"? If you don't rewind much further back than a mere couple thousand years B.C., it may *seem* that humans are patriarchal in nature. The answer is hidden in the same stories that have been propagated by the Genetypes for tens of thousands of years as humans migrated to the four corners of the planet, carrying the same stellar-religion blueprint in their backpacks— a religion that worshipped *females*.

The Egyptian religion was *matriarchal*, headed by "Nut" (pronounced "newt") as goddess of the cosmos and sky. On the ceilings of preserved ancient Egyptian temples you will see paintings of The Sky Goddess, Nut, swallowing the sun in the west and giving birth to the sun in the east, and passing through her at night. Following a theory I touched on in Part One, was the ancient migration of humans a sun-following quest to touch Nut, tens of thousands of years before she was painted on ceilings of Egyptian temples? Later on I shall give you evidence of such. In any case, the point is that for at least 95% of our genetic memory imprints, we saw a *goddess* as the primary redeemer, and, according to the principle of genetic inertia, deep down we still do.

The ancient Egyptians were acutely aware that civilization is a fragile veneer pasted over our lower, animalistic selves, and The Big Bad Wolf et al. we see so commonly in lasting folk tales is a legacy of this awareness, a metaphor of what lies "out there" if we don't stick to the correct fork in the road of the higher self of the human animal, if we don't maintain *balance*. Our oldest myths often point to this common warning for society: when The Masculine is out of balance with The Feminine, society shall ultimately *be lost*.

The Higher Love

At least at an individual level, then, let's take the fork in the road of the higher self to The Higher Love, for personal joy and to contribute to the greater good. How can we attain this higher love? To attain a goal, we must know what that goal is, what true love looks like, but how do we describe the indescribable? Interestingly, the default descriptor used by humans in conditions of extreme awe that cannot be defined is "*God.*" Anything beyond "God" is an attempt to describe feelings from an abstract dimension, a place that transcends the logical and the linear that defies coherent use of language.

Something in the meeting of the eyes goes deeper than any other contact, and there is suddenly nobody else in the room. The two of you connect as if magnets helplessly drawn together, a smell, a sense, *you somehow know each other yet you are strangers.* This is somehow a *re*union. Is it a DNA match from centuries ago that replicates in the present? In any case, *it is written.* The lyrics of all the love songs you've heard suddenly make sense. You are permanently and constantly *in* love, feeling like a brick in the stomach. *True* love feels like an understatement, and lust is a mere gateway to a condition of what can only be described as a transcendent state of *dissolution* into one another, outside one another and space and time, the orgasm hitting the other's bloodstream as if injecting with a hallucinogenic, launching a mental voyage beyond the incidental physical act that just took place. It is life and death in the same moment (the French phrase for an orgasm is *Le Petit Mort or "The Little Death"*). The one who can "kill" you is the only one who can resurrect you. This can supersede your purpose as a bliss state, irrelevant of Genetypes, flaws, and nurtures, and you *have no choice* but to accept the fact that your dying breath will be spent kissing this person on the lips, to feel The Energy flow between you one last (?) time.

Many people will dismiss what I just described as an unobtainable ideal, at least on a lasting basis, but this is because many people have unwittingly closed themselves off to this higher state of awareness, allowing their lower self to unconsciously amble down the wrong fork in the road, growing increasingly bitter with each grueling step of what becomes a negative feedback loop. The Metaphysical elevates the physical. Think of the times when you met someone you ended up loving *and* before one or both of you unconsciously sabotaged the relationship. Chances are it was when you felt happy with your life at the time, when you were at one with The Energy Field, *when you were closer to your higher self*. Walk through a busy street today and most people appear so unconscious that they look straight through you as if you're a ghost, let alone being open to this heightened state of awareness.

If "love" is interchangeable with "God," then God is good. Joyful transcendence through *equal* union is the path chosen by your higher self, and hidden in your ancient genes is the gateway to this dimension; you just have to walk through it. Let us now discuss your romantic relationships and Genetypal compatibility with this principle firmly in mind, and reclaim Paradise.

Genetypes in Relationships

A popularized line from the film *Forrest Gump* goes, "Mama always said life's like a box of chocolates; you never know what you're gonna get." But don't you just read the menu under the chocolate box to see what "you're gonna get"? When it comes to relationships, with Genetypal awareness you have such a menu: all the Genetypes are listed in Part Two, so you're either in a relationship with one of them already or are trying to choose one. Any belief outside of this is a nurtured fantasy.

When it comes to Genetypal reality in relationships, it's a harsh but simple affair; if you don't like the spots on a leopard, you have two choices: *learn* to like the spots, or choose another animal. A person's true self, their Genetype, is set in stone, and even those resilient, nurtured personality overlays such as "A-Type" and "Generational" aren't likely to go away with most people. I gave you a menu, now choose a dish from it or go hungry. Harder to do in an existing relationship, but nonetheless, it's time to take it or leave it because whining about it is no longer an option if you seek happiness.

The Genetype menu may also give you peace in an existing relationship if it stops you seeing the neighbor's grass as greener, and it may expose any extramarital affair for what it is. It may reignite your relationship and take it to new heights that may even include true love now that the veil is lifted on who you truly both are. But that realization may also destroy what was left of your relationship as you appreciate that it wasn't you simply imagining the disaster, kicking yourself for not paying attention to your gut in earlier years. Either way, you shall have truth, and the truth shall set you free.

We will shortly break out into a relationship section for each Genetype, listed by existing and new relationship considerations, so let's discuss that broadly to begin with. First, existing relationships.

Let's not confuse cynicism with realism. A great deal of relationship strife today is the result of modern culture—with its celebrity magazines, Grimm Brothers fairy tales, and "The *Best* of The Joneses" social media page—clashing with reality and the inevitable disappointment that ensues. Every contemporary fairy tale ends at the wedding, and there is no *Cinderella 2: The Bullshit*. So, especially after kissing so many frogs, there is disappointment when a newly complacent "Price Charming" farts, can't find anything, and generally acts like an ass. Likewise, when a newly complacent "Cinderella" trades in her ball gown for sweat pants, too weary from car line and soccer practice to "dance," The Prince is disappointed. For the sake of survival in ancient times, the human brain is a comparing engine, and in the instance of a relationship it's comparing initial fantasy with subsequent reality, and when the glass slipper doesn't fit, we see our partner as the villain.

Choosing correctly at the fork in the road isn't a one-and-done deal; it's a conscious daily effort. Many people lament about how good their relationship was "in the beginning," but it only deteriorated because they didn't make that conscious daily choice at the fork. I initially learned the hard way that few things will challenge you more or give you so many opportunities to grow as living with a romantic partner. Complacency is the mortal enemy of relationships because it's the gateway to lack of consciousness, and that is the realm of the lower self. Stress, hunger, fatigue, sickness, and intoxicants strip the outer layers of our brains down to what is essentially a reptilian core, the mindless animal within that coaxes us toward the lower path, and people in relationships will inevitably encounter such times. The ups and downs of life are what makes an *Authentic Life Experience*, or ALE as I call it, that when shared makes us stronger. Share an ALE; it's good for you.

Assuming you have some Genetypal compatibility and you are both still interested, there is a way to retrace your steps and make the correct choice at the fork. In the Disney film *Frozen*, the heroine, *Elsa,* joyously sings "Let It Go" as she locks herself away in an ice castle. If you wish an existing relationship to survive, you will first have to *let it go* instead of merely singing about it, and invite your partner in from the cold you banished them to. There are no in-betweens, in or out, *unconditionally*. The magic of reconciliation comes from forgiveness, understanding, and realism.

After you get out the way of yourself and are open to letting the past go, gift a copy of this book to your partner and read it together. Next, discover what Genetype you both are. Knowing each other so well can be a great tool to help find each other's Genetype and nurtures, and *if this is done in a constructive way* it could reignite your relationship *immediately.* You could facilitate and witness each other's rebirth, and what bond could be more powerful than that? Revealed to each other with fresh eyes, at least you now see who this person truly is, and you appreciate that nobody is perfect when you appreciate that all Genetypes have faults. This is powerful because suddenly all the times you asked yourself why a partner acts a certain way become clear, and you realize *that's just who they are*, and you stop holding it against them and start forgiving them (even if it means letting them go). This alone may knock walls down. Respect their Genetype as you expect yours to be respected, and remember that we each have a part to play in The Global Tribe. Now that you know each other at a new and true level of intimacy, what next?

You have a child clinging onto you, a lower self, *and so does your partner*. Engage your higher self and speak to your partner's higher self. Make a pact to *give* energy to each other's higher self instead of your lower selves constantly *taking* energy from each other. How can you give this energy? As Billy Joel sang, "Tell her about it." It's all in the lyrics of that old song; just interchange "her/she" with "him/he" if you're a woman because both men and women need to feel loved and be told "about it" by their partners. The crucial part Billy Joel missed out was what "*language*" you should use to tell her/him about it.

In Gary Chapman's insightful book, *The 5 Love Languages*, he explains how different people show love and wish to receive love in different ways. There is evidently something in our genes that dictates how we communicate love. Akin to aligning with a person's Genetypal nature, the book shows that if we don't express love to a partner in the way *they* express love, *our* expression of love literally falls on deaf ears, as if we are speaking a foreign language, despite our own belief that, speaking in our own love language, we *are* expressing love. The Five Love Languages are Acts of Service, Gifts, Words of Affirmation, Quality Time, and Physical Touch. We usually like all these "languages," but one will usually be dominant, much as a Genetype has a Dominant Driver. For anyone (usually male) who struggles with "sweet talk," the good news is that only one in five people actually need it.

Find out which love language your partner speaks (which is usually the thing they complain most about not getting), and start speaking to them accordingly, even if *you* speak a different love language than them. Next, you can massively boost Chapman's great work by customizing your partner's love language according to their Genetype. For example, two different Genetypes who both have

"Gifts" as their love language will likely have completely different ideas about what constitutes a gift. This complication that Chapman refers to as "love language *dialects*" is solved by customizing a love language according to Genetype. Ask: "How could I serve/gift/touch/praise/quality time my partner's specific *Genetype*?" *This is incredibly powerful*, and you should expect a dramatic and instant response from your partner *if* they still love you. If your partner speaks a different love language *and/or dialect* to you, make this a daily habit, keeping a journal to make notes on what works and what doesn't. Just hope it's not too late. If this all sounds like too much hassle for you, then you know it's too late or that it was never true love in the first place.

Next, let's consider finding new relationships. If you're unattached, you are a privileged reader because you get to use all this knowledge to now choose a partner wisely, armed with Genetype awareness. With Genetypes in mind, I trust you now appreciate that nobody is perfect, but somebody is perfect for you. There is no Prince/Princess Charming. This book gave you a list of the seven male and seven female Genetypes, and they all have faults; you just need to decide which flaws are deal breakers and choose your ideal Genetype.

Next, find that Genetype. Just as nurtures were obscuring the view of your Genetype, so will they when you attempt to identify another person's Genetype, but with practice you'll be able to cut through a person's nurtures to identify their Genetype with only a few questions. Even before you get to the questions, with practice you'll notice that appearances and energy can be distinctly seen between certain Genetypes before they've said a word. Once engaged in conversation, the trick is to identify the Dominant Driver as quickly as possible, using a process of elimination to get it down from seven possibilities to just one or two. Asking what a person's favorite film/book is and why can tell you a lot if you're listening carefully. Asking what they love to do or dream about doing is another good question. Watch closely for the moments when the conversation makes their eyes widen because that's when you can peer into their soul (a.k.a. Genetype).

When you appreciate that a person's Genetype defines them and therefore what spending a lifetime with them would look like, correctly assessing a person's Genetype on the first date could *instantly* tell you whether you'd want to marry them or not. Just don't say as much yet, lest they think you're a psycho, but that's ultra-efficient dating!

Ignore peer pressure and don't compare yourself to others. The right person is worth waiting for, so smash your rose-tinted glasses and think objectively about what will be one of the most important decisions of your life. Biological clocks, milestone birthdays, and hounding relatives (other Genetypes with other agendas) are hazards that can skew your vision at this fork in the road. Don't succumb.

True love between two people should become a growing tree, and hurt is a mere storm that sways the branches, but not the trunk of this tree. And that trunk is true, reciprocating, unconditional love, rooted deep into your heart and soul, and even if this tree was violently cut down, the roots remain forever. You can love a person so much that you'd let them go if it meant they would be happy, even though it would destroy you. True love is from someone who loves you for who you really are. Accept nothing less.

Genetype Breakout: Mirror, Mirror

First, some notes before we break out into Genetypes. Because all Genetypes have inherent faults, every Genetypal match has an inherent "fault line" that will become an earthquake under pressure unless the couple is conscious of it. The trick is to understand that dramatic Genetypal differences don't have to be destructive; they can give one another a healthy balance if there is awareness. I've refrained from possible matchmaking because I've found it can spark insecurity within existing relationships and because there is no perfect match, so I will leave possible matches for you to figure out. Genetypes are *not* necessarily male-female paired according to numbers (such as MG-1 paired with FG-1, or FG-4 paired with MG-4). The coding is entirely incidental and random.

So, now the concept of Mr. or Mrs. "Perfect" is replaced with Genetypal reality, my focus in this section is a closer look at your Genetype's dark side and the negative effect it can have on your relationships. True, you can't change your nature, but you must *awaken* to its shadow *and* to your partner's. So I offer you the following keys to consciousness in the context of relationship success. Awareness of your inherent weaknesses won't make them go away, but consciousness of them brings them to heel and encourages you to consider the impact of them on those you love. Also, these keys to consciousness are designed to help you grow and make your Genetype more complete.

FG-1

Keys to consciousness:
Your key to consciousness is to become more introspective, finding your own identity separate from your children or others in need, learning to let go, stopping worrying so much, and loving yourself as much as you love others.

Existing Relationships:
You can go to extremes of helping others to the point of martyrdom, a dark lining on your silver cloud, which can irritate others. Someone who truly loves you wants you to be happy, so your constant worrying will cause them pain and despair, and that is the very last thing you of all people want. Focusing your compassion at least equally on your partner instead of mostly on your children could be the hardest challenge because you instinctively lock on to those most in need of care. But try to see that the marriage staying intact is of the best interests of your children's care and happiness, and you must see the bigger picture. There is a balance to helping others and helping yourself and your partner. Don't treat your partner as a patient; treat them as a lover. Do not let a partner take advantage of your kind nature by constantly draining you or needlessly occupying you.

New Relationships:
A Genetype who enjoys being looked after works well, but don't allow a dysfunctional lower self of another be seen as a wounded soldier to fix.

FG-2
Keys to consciousness:
Your key to consciousness is balancing work and play and embracing your feminine side instead of seeing it as weakness. Develop an "off switch" for your personal life, and know when and how to relax and reconnect with your femininity. Not everything in life is a competition.

Existing Relationships:
You can be as stubborn as you can be proud. Your desire to win (arguments) at all costs is problematic in maintaining any healthy relationship where sometimes one has to let things go or concede

a point even when they don't believe it, just for the sake of peace. Friction with others can be a factor if you become competitive in a Beat-the-Joneses fashion, especially if your partner feels financially strained as a result.

New Relationships:
Understandably, you're attracted to powerful types, and in the event that you're unable to work, you would stand behind such a person. A male who isn't intimidated or emasculated by female power will be most harmonious for you. Don't be tempted into a relationship with a controllable male just because it means an easy victory for you over men, because that could end up frustrating you and leaving you unfulfilled.

FG-3
Keys to consciousness:
Your key to consciousness is not taking the world's problems on your shoulders and embracing more of a public life. Full moons affect everyone to a degree but few more than you, so be mindful of the lunar cycle.

Existing Relationships:
If already married, focus on your ability to bless a home with joy and compassion. But assert your need for occasional solitude, communicating that it's about your needs and that they should not take it personally. Explain that spontaneity is fun as well as routine, and teach your partner how to be more self-sufficient and to enjoy some solitude for themselves when you have yours. You shouldn't have to lose your identity by getting married, and your desire to please everyone and keep the peace makes you a potential victim for this, leading to your own stress that climaxes in a vicious snap that seems out of character for the usual kindness and calm you emanate.

New Relationships:
You will definitely not be happy with a possessive or controlling
partner because you need your space and solitude. There are one
or two male Genetypes you'll notice that could be a good fit. Bear
in mind that, regrettably, many males instinctively want to control/
own/dominate a woman, and you won't take kindly to that, however alluring the freedom of being financially supported may be.

FG-4

Keys to consciousness:
Your key to consciousness is accepting a spiritual death: the reality
that looks *do* fade and to selflessly pass on your gift to The Tribe,
instead embracing your creativity and intellect as you grow old
gracefully while retaining your femininity.

Existing Relationships:
Be aware how draining it can be for a partner to keep the spotlight
on you, attend to dramas, and to keep a steady flow of original
compliments coming. Your tendency to block out the parts of
reality you don't want to be true can make communication an issue,
and this is crucial for any relationship to work. You can be manip-
ulative, but doing this to someone you truly love? The enlightened
and experienced version of your Genetype has learned to neutralize
the threat other females perceive from you by paying them compliments and building up their sexual confidence—your key to gaining
and keeping female friends—although the spotlight usually isn't
big enough for two of your Genetype in a group.

New Relationships:
You need to find someone who sees you for who you really are
under the surface, takes you seriously, and doesn't treat you as a
sex object. You're inclined to fall into the trap of being a mistress,
the proverbial "other woman" who clings onto the hope that this

time he really will leave his wife for you, but he probably never will, and you could lose valuable years waiting.

FG-5

Keys to consciousness:

Your key to consciousness is appreciating that you can't save everyone, and understanding that causes can take generations to win the day. Your late Genetypal predecessors knew this and passed the baton to you, as you shall do the same to the Genetypes that follow you. Also, understand that not all threats you perceive to the vulnerable are actual threats, so be sure not to deliver "friendly fire."

Existing Relationships:

It's as if you're on the edge of your seat a lot of the time, sometimes striking out at perceived threats to the vulnerable without justification, and this will take its toll on the wrong match. You can be competitive and opinionated, perhaps even becoming boastful, stubborn, and unbalanced in the process, and a relationship struggles with someone who always needs to win a fight. You want and need female friends, and now I hope you can see that not all females will have the same priorities as you, so there's no point in getting annoyed with them because of this; it doesn't mean they don't respect a cause.

New Relationships:

You're obviously going to be more compatible with Genetypes less inclined to overdominance and patriarchy, and you should be able to spot those now. You may end up with more male friends and multiple relationships or marriages, and you're often more of a living-together type than marrying type.

FG-6

Keys to consciousness:
Your key to consciousness is confronting your fear of being independent. Also see the lengthy explanation in the previous section on your purpose because your key to consciousness is a journey of transformation.

Existing Relationships:
Pre-awakening: Most people loathe drama, so be sure to keep this in check or to transform, or to pick a partner who doesn't mind it or even enjoys it. Be mindful of your darkest side emerging when your fears are triggered. Such traits include: excessive attention seeking, tantrums when others don't pick up after you, entitled behavior, getting into trouble with everyone close to you constantly worrying about you as if a wild teenager.

Post-awakening: Change can scare a partner, and a dramatic change awaits you. They need to understand this and know it doesn't affect the relationship. Try to involve them.

New Relationships:
Pre-awakening: Your childlike vulnerability projects a damsel in distress image that domineering men find appealing, to protect you but perhaps also control you, and loss of freedom is a problem for you, so there is a paradox.

Post-awakening: Your choice of partner will likely change from someone who is a safety net for you to someone who helps you become a safety net for others.

FG-7

Keys to consciousness:
Your key to consciousness is separating your happiness from that of your partner's, and not letting them get the upper hand or becoming a slave to their ego. A perpetual source of suffering for you is the perception of not being a good partner simply because the other person is unhappy. Not that you shouldn't listen and help, but their unhappiness is *their* issue and may be an inherent problem that only they can fix.

Existing Relationships:
You want to be the quintessential perfect wife and to make your partner happy, but not for them as much as *yourself* so you can lead and rule *together*. Any perception that they're striving for superiority over you or taking advantage of your idolization can cause a tantrum that may, ironically, involve walking out on them for a few days. So you're far from being a doormat, especially if your partner is unfaithful. Easily angered and not easily rattled, the phrase "Hell hath no fury like a woman scorned" was a generalization; it should've said, "Hell hath no fury like an FG-7 scorned." Better a partner doesn't trigger this in you, but be mindful of the severe, possibly irreparable damage such a trait can cause, however much you think, "Well, they made me do it by acting that way."

New Relationships:
There can be only one lucky person, so be careful not to fall into the classic FG-7 trap of gravitating toward a childlike type. Now you have the Genetype menu. *Choose wisely . . .*

MG-1

Keys to consciousness:

You won't want to hear this, but the path to consciousness and completion is to get in touch with your emotions, become more flexible, and not try to be in control of everything, separating personal life from professional life. Accept that part of the human condition means that not everything revolves around logic. There is a spiritual side of life to at least be open to exploring; see it as a research project.

Existing Relationships:

Your dark side is arrogance, a very unattractive quality, so be mindful of this. Stubbornness means not conceding when necessary, and that's a problem. Being married to your career can make your partner feel more like a mistress and make your children see you as a distant uncle. Use the Genetype guide to identify your partner and the structure and logic behind what they're doing and why. I know your head is constantly yearning to be at the office instead of the home, but force yourself to make one spontaneous and out-of-character act with your family and see where it takes you.

New Relationships:

You have the Genetype menu, and now the chaotic world of dating and personalities is clear.

MG-2

Keys to consciousness:

Learn to connect with people, muster more acceptance of the human condition, and to triumph at one great love in your life.

Existing Relationships:

You occasionally go on a vocal rampage against people you see as epitomizing the mess out there, and this can cause tension. Your partner is probably the one to work at the relationship, understanding that what you do is important and requires concentration, but bear that in mind and don't take it for granted. If they don't understand you, then educate them and learn about them too. Ideally, this partner becomes a valuable part of your rich inner world and someone to bounce your ideas off. Be mindful of bearing grudges, not showing emotion, not communicating, negativity, and vocal rampages.

New Relationships:
No man is an island, not even you, but it's vital that you have a certain type of partner who can integrate to your lifestyle in a harmonious way for you both. Eventually, the loneliness will become too much to bear, and when that time comes, be sure to study the Genetypes carefully and search for someone who also requires solitude or who is absent a great deal for work, who is intellectual or who appreciates the deeper and spiritual side of life, who isn't particularly sociable, and is low maintenance.

MG-3

Keys to consciousness:
Master the art of counting to three before you speak, getting between your knee-jerk feelings and your mouth. I know you don't mean the heated words, but perception is reality, and it's hard for people to believe you didn't mean it. Also, learn to react (or not) to how a situation actually is, not how you imagine it to be. This will require a great deal of practice and mindfulness.

Existing Relationships:
The good news: you're the same Genetype as rock stars. The bad news: you're the same Genetype as rock stars. Passion and fury alike flow through you, ever present in varying degrees, but consciousness of this fact is half the battle to not letting it ruin your life. In ancient

times, your unexpected bursts of rage would've been respected and revered as simply the gods being angry and using you as their microphone, but in modern society this is seen as unacceptable. If trapped in a relationship that's soured, now you know who's likely to blame (yes, you). Your creative strength is your relationship weakness, ultimately. You can be sensitive to criticism, attaching every comment to your creativity. You can be self-centered, only seeing your own problems, the *perceived* intensity of them stealing all your focus, which is a shame because you love your family deeply. Sometimes you wish The Muse would leave you in peace so you could be more present with them. You can become vengeful if wronged or if you *imagine* you're wronged.

New Relationships:
Regardless of Genetype, unless you learn to control your emotions and understand the hurt your throwaway words can cause, you will be locked in a perpetual loop of loveless or broken relationships unless you find someone who understands the issue (that it really isn't you speaking at the time of the lash out) and loves you unconditionally for who you are and what you represent.

MG-4

Keys to consciousness:
Experience the rewards of romantic commitment to only one person and exploration of a metaphysical place you've yet to touch.

Existing Relationships:
See Part Three. If you could become a faithful and committed partner, you would be most women's dream. Men can make good friends as well as women, although in some bad examples their homophobic demeanor or success-driven mentalities may have driven you away. People may initially find your dreams and grand plans alluring, but if they don't materialize, they can see you as a fraud or a flake, which was not your intention.

New Relationships:
You know the drill, only now you're awake and empowered. Study the menu very carefully, choose *one*, and go get them . . .

MG-5

Keys to consciousness:
Don't forsake your good qualities, but do appreciate the consequences of your nature, both on yourself and others. Awareness isn't growing up, it's simply opening your eyes, especially when it comes to those closest to you.

Existing Relationships:
"Help me find my shadow," Peter Pan said to Wendy. You have a dark side usually only as far as perceived by a romantic partner because such a relationship usually requires the one thing you're afraid of: getting tied down. A child is innocent, curious, loving, and fun—that's what I told you in your initial Genetype description. Now I must tell you that a child is also amoral, self-congratulating, flighty, and entitled. Be aware of this and how it impacts relationships and friendships. You may also need to be told something several times before it sinks in. You confuse partners when you come across as unreliable, flaky, or tardy with arrangements, not understanding that you simply need space and freedom, that you lose track of time, that you can be gone for days without warning, so explain you don't mean disrespect by it and be aware of the impact.

New Relationships:
If you end up in a committed relationship, and that's a big "if," you will need someone to take charge in a parental sense *and not mind doing so.* This partner must truly complete you and give you the freedom you need without it compromising the relationship, and this can be a tall order. Study the Genetypes carefully for a suitable life partner, if at all.

MG-6

Keys to consciousness:
Connect with your mind as well as your body. You must learn
self-control and spirituality as the samurai and Jedi had to.

Existing Relationships:
Be mindful of getting sucked into unnecessary conflict, because your
ancient Genetype is sometimes ill suited to the more diplomatic
solutions required in contemporary life. Your tendency to constantly feel threatened and to react physically could be a problem
domestically (and professionally, especially if a police officer,
which is a common career choice for your Genetype), and you
must be able to disconnect within the home and not be so quick
to fly off the handle or get physical. Learn the Female Genetypes
and learn more about why people act the way they do, and count
to three before reacting. You must also sympathize with the fact
that your children, particularly any son of yours, will likely not be
the same Genetype as you, and you're in danger of damaging his
impressionable self-esteem at a young age if he appears less of a
"man" to you.

New Relationships:
You're a spontaneous man who will thrive with a spontaneous
partner, ideally one who also wants an especially protective type
(to take care of all matters as well as physical). You enjoy sex and
the thrill of the chase, so choose accordingly from the Genetypes;
you'll quickly notice how unsuitable some of them are for you.

MG-7

Keys to consciousness:
Attainment of consciousness requires a sense of duality, but you
won't entertain that because you see emotions as weakness. But

if you can see the problem with that mentality and how it affects other people, then you're *already* on the road to completion and consciousness.

Existing Relationships:
The only thing that can make self-confident people lose respect from others is when their confidence struts over the knife edge that divides it from arrogance. You feel incomplete without a partner at your side, but if you try to reign over them, *you ultimately will lose them* mentally and/or physically. You must treat your partner with the same respect you wish to be treated, which is mighty, or all is lost. Rule as equals or Camelot falls. It's crucial that you do not belittle your partner as if they were one of your "subjects." You feel entitled to a double life, so if that leads you to take a mistress, don't be surprised when you get caught. Otherwise, until you learn humility, no relationship can thrive, and the same fate as Captain Ahab from *Moby Dick* awaits you: ultimately destroyed by a quest to conquer what dared offend you, even life itself. Don't be a prisoner of pride. Regarding family and friends, you sometimes deserve the ring that you require others to kiss, but without power and/or money supporting your claim on a "kingdom," (the) people eventually see through "The Emperor's Clothes," and a cruel emperor would be quickly disregarded. But there is also spiritual wealth, and this can never be taken from you.

New Relationships:
You've figured out a suitable Genetype choice by now or you aren't the man I thought.

Happy Families

Our need for love is also about belonging (to a tribe), and friends and family can give us that feeling or take it away. We can't choose family, but blood can be thicker than water when it matters most, and remember that your family is made up of different Genetypes, some of which will inherently be about as compatible as oil and water; but remember that we need both oil and water in our society. People today talk much about "celebrating diversity," yet I don't see much evidence of it within families and social circles when it comes to Genetypal diversity.

There is nothing like having children. Pay close attention to your Genetype and purpose to ensure such a serious commitment is compatible with your life map. A child's love for a parent is inherent and unconditional, primarily for hardwired survival reasons. Your children may resemble you physically and they may inherit traits from you or the other parent, but underneath that they have a Genetype, just as you do, and that Genetype may be the same as yours, or it may not, and their Genetype may or may not clash with yours. But proceed with caution before assigning children a Genetype. Better to stay open minded and to watch for clues, and then use a process of trial and error instead of snap judgments or assigning them the Genetype most likeable to you. It's easier to spot a child's Genetype when they're younger (or if you accurately recall when they were younger), before nurture and society pours rubble on them as they hit the double digits. Let's take a couple of examples of using the power of Genetypal awareness with children.

Adapting consequences for bad behavior to each Genetype is effective. This is why some children shrug at certain punishments or can be badly traumatized by them, and somewhere in the middle is the right disciplinary approach to your child's Genetype. An

MG-6 (Protector) child, who is inherently quick to the fists instead of finding his words, does not need Ritalin or a psychiatrist. Most of all, he doesn't need to see physical discipline (which would only condone his physical expression). What he needs is Genetypal understanding. Incidentally, *The 5 Love Languages* are just as applicable to children, especially when customized to their Genetype.

Don't be surprised by FG-3 or MG-3 children being oversensitive to people's energy and/or struggling to articulate fast enough what The Energy Field is trying to say through them. You can understand most children's behavior when you know their Genetype.

A friend of mine who is an FG-7 (Matriarch) has two daughters, and she complained to me about how she couldn't interest her eldest in any after-school activities that she'd offered this child. After observing this daughter, it was fairly clear she was an FG-4 (Creative), one of the easier Genetypes to spot, and very different to her mother's domineering Genetype, but I kept an open mind.

"Did you try acting classes?" I said.

"No. I would never be interested in something like that," she said.

"Ah. But your daughter might. Take her to acting or dancing classes, anything that involves the performing arts. See how she does."

Evidently the mother took my advice, and a few weeks later she profusely thanked me for "bringing her daughter to life, as if by magic." It's not magic; it's simply knowing Genetypes. Lots of little girls would like acting classes, but only an FG-4's world would be rocked so much by them.

One simple act of understanding toward a child can change your life, that child's life, and perhaps even the world, because them being purpose-driven from such a young age could lead to great things. Embracing your purpose and giving your gift to the world is your love. Helping others do the same is your love and their emancipation.

Children have their own path, their own soul, and I don't believe it's up to parents to decide on a child's purpose, some parents taking it to something resembling bullying. You don't need a doctorate in psychology to know many adults are unhappy and stuck in a career they hate because their parents consciously or unconsciously told them that was the correct path. Your children are not an extension of you and your own ambitions, or a second chance for you to claim the dreams you wanted; the dream you should've followed may or may not be that of your child's. Don't become a disruptive voice of nurture in that child's corridor of choices later on in their life. Don't throw rubble on their beautiful plant; throw water on it.

You'll be a much more effective and rewarded parent for considering your child's Genetypal definition of "success" than yours or society's. In some cases, like possibly that of MG-5 (Freedom) or FG-3 (Connection with Spiritual), success may simply be to live in a camper in the woods. What you see as failure, your child's Genetype could see as fulfillment. Your job as a parent is to give your children wings, *but those wings likely belong to birds of a different feather than you.*

The Ashes of Eden

As an unbalanced relationship drifts off course one degree at a time so it's barely noticeable until it's too late, so too did humanity gradually drift away from its ancient and hard-won wisdom that the first civilizations like Egypt and Sumer inherited and articulated. The evidence is in the myths of the day.

Around 3,000 B.C., violent animal-herding nomads, who worshipped male warrior-gods such as Zeus, infringed on agrarian civilizations like Egypt that were fertility-based, hence goddess based, and began to influence the culture, making it steadily drift away from goddess worship and what it stood for, altering the balance. A similar thing happened when Aztecs took power in Latin America, leaving the images of human sacrifice we now associate with that culture.

Despite The Goddess remaining a potent figure in ancient Greek mythology, as well as that mythology inheriting many morals of balance from Egypt, the shift was barely noticeable, but the seeds of patriarchy were planted. Zeus, the male king of gods, only became so after overthrowing Gaia, the first goddess. And then his goddess wife, Hera, became the Egyptian fertility goddess ("Nut") equivalent but moved over to be at Zeus's side, the couple still ruling together, but now she was slightly lower down on the hierarchy.

Greek mythology unashamedly then tells how Zeus effectively stole all his powers by mating with various goddesses either through rape or trickery, giving birth to other gods and goddesses such as Apollo and Artemis. Then came what would become a fatal blow for The Feminine, even if unintended, as Pandora, the first human woman, failed to resist opening the forbidden box and thus unleashed all that was evil about humanity. From Eve to Snow White, women would then be misconstrued as being too weak to avoid temptation, leaving chaos in their wake, when it is men who are generally more inclined to infidelity, the likely result of ruling class males projecting their own faults onto females.

The Goddess was now on the path to something worse than inequality; she was on the path to vilification, while Zeus's lust binge and blood lust was condoned. This set in motion the pattern for women to be blamed for men's ego issues and the resultant destruction, from society being out of balance. The moral of Homer's famous story in *The Iliad* was misconstrued at some point; it wasn't Helen of Troy's beautiful face that launched a thousand warships, it was the ego of a jealous and spiteful king who sent thousands of men to their death all because he treated his wife like a piece of meat and didn't care for the consequences or admit being wrong.

When the Hebrews sacked Canaan and found a statue of a goddess with a serpent, our prized ancient symbol of rebirth, it was torn down and condemned as an "abomination."

Ancient Rome inherited its mythology from Greece, renamed the gods and goddesses, and built an empire that, for all the civilization it brought to the world, also brought death and destruction. Rome was built on a myth of two belligerent brothers, Romulus and Remus, who were raised by wolves, with Romulus eventually killing Remus—man literally killing his own brother. Rome was forged by violence and ended in decadence and disease, crumbling not long after converting to Christianity. What shreds of The Goddess that remained were scattered into the aptly named Dark Ages, along with the ashes of Rome.

Our most ancient lesson was lost: the consequence of letting our lower selves rise to prominence and of allowing patriarchs to move us out of balance. We lost Paradise when we lost our connection with "Goddess." We took the wrong fork in the road. This was our Original Sin.

part five

CONTAINS
REAL FRUIT

Running on Empty

"Whoever severs himself from Mother Earth and her flowing sources of life goes into exile." – Emma Goldman.

Your life map is irrelevant if you die crossing it, so let us put Genetypes to one side for this part of the book and deal with a crucial issue that doesn't care what kind of person you are. Is there anything hidden in our ancient genes that can help our health and longevity? What does your new life map say about lifestyle?

The threat to your health is an invisible, creeping one that our ancient genes are ill equipped for. We are unconscious time travelers. Because of genetic inertia, our bodies are still attempting to live off the land that we've known for 2.5 million years but instead have to live off a new land where "Contains REAL Fruit!" is advertised as a unique benefit. Your very survival depends on your ability to adapt to this strange land our ancient bodies have found themselves in. All Genetypes share the same biology (apart from one important difference I'll speak about), and when it comes to health, I'm not asking you to change who you are, I'm asking you to *remember* who we are, in the biological sense. Survive, for you have purposeful work ahead of you.

Our ancient senses are being deceived by synthetic illusions, creating a double impact of not only depriving ourselves of the goodness, but replacing it with badness. For example, licorice root has many health benefits including being an anti-inflammatory, but it tastes bad. So nineteenth-century British confectioners wrapped it in sugar as a way of getting children to eat it. Legacies of this practice are seen today in the form of licorice twists (and "Licorice Allsorts" candies in the UK), but if you're expecting to find licorice in the contemporary version's ingredients, you can expect disappointment, because postwar food manufacturers figured out that by adding artificial licorice *flavoring* instead of *real* licorice, they could make the product taste the same only cheaper and/or sell it to the consumer for cheaper. The consumer doesn't read ingredients labels, they just want their licorice twists, so everyone seems happy.

The artificial additive isn't toxic in small doses—few things are—but over time, with every food undergoing the same deception, especially when packaged for convenience, the toxicity builds in our bodies, and by the time we see a symptom, it's the proverbial tip of an iceberg. Licorice candy only is one small example, but it applies to almost every processed item you see in your grocery store. Pick your poison, and to our bodies that belong to our lengthy past, it literally *is* a slow and insidious poisoning. The human body didn't survive and evolve for millions of years without becoming resilient and reparable, but it can only take so much, especially when nothing of value is being fed to it.

We've come to accept that people die of various conditions as a part of life, but the *rate* at which this is happening with certain conditions over the last fifty years is climaxing in an epidemic of global proportions that's hurtling up our blind side, and by the time we all wake up to the crisis, I fear it will be too late.

We are slowly committing suicide in a fashion that barely differentiates us from the mass suicides of a cult, with ignorance and denial as our gods, our cult leaders corrupted by money. In the time it took you to read the previous paragraph, someone in America died of a heart-related disease. In a quarter of cases, the first symptom of a heart attack is death.

According to The World Health Organization's 2016 data, cardiovascular disease has accelerated dramatically in the previous decade alone, after a steady rise for the preceding fifty years. The total worldwide number of deaths caused by cardiovascular disease in 2016 was 17.65 million, now dwarfing the commonly perceived number-one threat of cancer by 8.72 million deaths. Road incidents were only 1.34 million, and violent conflict a relatively low 120,000. Fire scored 130,000, and terrorism 30,000. A regular inspection of such data helps one apportion concerns accordingly when it comes to health and safety, but try telling that to the three-hundred-pound, jingoistic gun nuts who obsess about terrorist attacks instead of their belt size. Over 40% of Americans are now classified as obese, and over 50% are on at least one prescription drug. Fifteen hundred people die of cancer in America every single day. Please don't let ignorance and denial make you the next statistic.

To add to this, our body's ancient way of telling us something is steadily wrong with our diet—fatigue—is drowned out by caffeine addictions. The Dietary Dictators ("My diet's better than your diet! Follow *my* rules!") aren't helping and are merely adding to the confusion that's causing the mass population to do the absolute worst thing anyone can do in the face of danger: *nothing.*

The people we turn to for help, the medical establishment, are focusing on symptoms instead of causes, primarily because they're sponsored by pharmaceutical companies who simply want to sell drugs. As an airline pilot, I was trained in simulators to look for the root cause of a problem, not the symptoms of one. If several electrical warning lights come on at once, the generator has likely failed, so we should focus on the generator failure (cause) to fix all the other failures (symptoms). We are currently being overwhelmed by a variety of "warning lights," not only cancer and heart disease, but everything from dementia to diabetes, and we need to look for the *root cause* of the alarming rise of *all* these problems.

There is a common denominator that nobody can deny: our bodies are becoming more prone to malfunction than at any time in the last hundred years, particularly since the 1950s and the birth of processed and "fast" foods, a coinciding relationship that can no longer be ignored.

Consciousness of thought and action is now an imperative for our species, for its very survival in the matter of what we ingest and how we treat the ecosystem our food comes from.

My favorite use of The 80/20 Rule is to derive 80% of the benefit from only 20% of the effort required, so let's apply that method to health. This part of our life map is an information jungle we will hack a path through with three simple concepts that are hidden in our ancient genes: The Gorging Gene, Ancient Blood, and Energy Field Alignment.

The Gorging Gene

Thanks to an ingenious evolution of human biology, our genetic programming tells us to consume foods that taste sweet, like ripe fruit, and to consume all we can when we have access to it because we don't know when we will have access to this energy supply again. Thanks to insulin, any surplus sugars we don't burn off at the time of consumption will be converted into fat storage to get us through the times when food is scarce. Today, this works against us as we walk down the candy aisle in the grocery store.

Watch people "free refill" their plastic barrels of soda at gas stations, on their way to the pharmacy to pick up insulin injections, all so their primal taste buds can be tricked into keeping the economic carousel running. The problem is that the food manufacturers have us all addicted to sugar, and it's hiding almost everywhere and where you least expect it. Yes, I said *addicted.* In controlled experiments, sugar has been proven to invoke the same brain responses as cocaine, and cocaine-addicted laboratory rats are even proven to prefer a sugar addiction to a cocaine addiction. In the absence of Sugar Rehab Clinics, we are going to have to create our own. Drug rehab is rough, but on the bright side, it will sound glamorous and celebrity-esque to tell people you're "in rehab."

I've heard some medical doctors sensationally "myth bust" that sugar doesn't cause diabetes and actually it's *fat* that does, and they're right, but they're also wrong because they're not explaining the whole picture. To explain, fat in the blood causes type 2 diabetes because the fat blocks sugar from supplying energy to muscle cells, so the sugar stays in the blood, leading to insulin resistance and diabetes. But here's the other part of the story: *the very purpose of insulin is to turn sugar into the fat that's causing the problem.* So, yes, sugar does lead to diabetes, but not directly.

A calorie isn't always a calorie from the point of view of gaining weight, a.k.a. fat storage. Some sugars are naturally in whole foods, and those aren't the problem; the problem is the *added* sugar in most processed foods we consume. Sugars that occur naturally in foods, such as fruit, when consumed in moderation don't have the same effect because the fiber in the whole food pulls the sugar into the digestive system, which is why it's better to blend fruits and vegetables, not press or squeeze them. Conversely, when you consume something like a soda (virtually pure and unnatural sugar in the form of high fructose corn syrup), the sugar hits the liver practically directly, triggering insulin production almost immediately with the subsequent conversion of it to stored fat. Carbohydrates consumed to a degree more than needed also get broken into sugar, which is still a sugar. There is no magic bullet; you just have to check in to rehab.

It's not about calories as much as spikes in insulin production. The higher the Glycemic Index of the food (G.I. Index), the more likely the insulin spike, and natural sugars such as honey are still sugars (not to discount their health benefits in small doses). When you consider the biology, you appreciate that it's also as much about the *rate* of consumption, so in theory you could enjoy a candy bar without much consequential fat storage, but the catch is that you'd need to take all day to eat it, crumbs at a time to avoid insulin spikes.

As a legacy of our ancient survival instincts, most human behavior can be linked back to pain avoidance, but in the modern setting this causes problems. One of the greatest hazards we face today is the moral one: "I want to eat what I want, and if I get sick my doctor should give me a pill." "If I'm comfortable in my body, it's okay to be chronically obese. Saying otherwise is unkind." Your doctor may well be more than happy to prescribe you all the pills you want, but you should know the risks, particularly of taking multiple drugs, and how the side effects can lead to you taking even more drugs. And it's basic medical fact that obesity is linked to all number of diseases, especially cardiovascular, and it is the greatest danger to society today, regardless of how it impacts an obese person's feelings. Denial and linguistic fascism will be no consolation when they cut an artery out of your leg and attach it to your heart, and people who tell us that it's okay to be obese have blood on their hands. Again, *truth doesn't care about being popular, but it does set you free.* In this case, truth saves your life.

Ancient Blood

Cast your mind back to those unfortunate times when you suffered from food poisoning. You could've eaten a wide variety of foods within the previous few days that might have caused it, but somehow you knew the specific food item that was the culprit. Not only biologically, but *psychically*, your gut knew which foods to stay away from for future consumption. This ancient instinct was hard won and remains in us today and in our sense of smell and our taste buds, an additional line of defense before consumption. This served humans well on their great migrations out of East Africa, helping them adapt to new environments.

The reason humans have different blood groups is because of our different stages of evolution in different parts of the world. As we spread out, the environment changed, so genetic mutation went to work. Our skin color adapted for optimum Vitamin D absorption and frostbite tolerance in less sunny areas than East Africa, and our digestive and immune systems adapted for the inevitable change in diet and germs. Digestive and immune systems depend on our blood, and so we now have the blood groups O, A, B, and AB. Just as success is a function of Genetypes, so is diet for blood groups.

The reason blood transfusion donors have to match the recipient's blood group is because of the marked differences in how blood groups react to different germs and foods. Because of genetic inertia, international trade, and modern-day migrations, your blood group may be receiving entirely inappropriate foods, resulting in weight and health problems. Even optimum types of exercise results have been linked to blood groups.

Following on the work of scientist Karl Landsteiner, in the 1950s another scientist named Arthur Mourant began the study of blood groups and diet and how they tie in with anthropology. This was continued by J. D'Adamo with his extremely detailed book, *Eat Right for Your Type.* In summary, O-type is the oldest blood group attributed more to the foraging ancestors before 10,000 B.C. A-type is attributed to the move to agrarian societies after 10,000 B.C. B-type dates between 15,000 B.C. and 10,000 B.C. AB-type is a modern mutation within the last 2,000 years.

This is not an exhaustive list of blood-appropriate foods, but enough to make you aware, get the general principle, and to begin further research:

O-type is best suited to meat and fish, root vegetables. This is the oldest group, so the menu is understandable and based on a higher stomach acid for digesting less cultivated foods. Foods of agriculture, such as dairy and grains and beans, are not best suited, hence gluten and lactose and soy intolerances are high in this group.

A-type is more agrarian in nature by history, so dairy and grains and a wider variety of vegetables than O-types are appropriate, including the more cultivated kinds than root based. With lower stomach acid than O-type, meat in moderation and more plant-based diets work better, including soy.

B-type is varied and a blend of both O and A, though usually more A, and with a particular liking to seafood.

AB is a total blend of A and B.

Diet books and plans may work well for one blood group but not for another, so the debates about which diet plan works is as flawed as Genetypes debating over what should be a person's Dominant Driver. The Dietary Dictators are particularly polarized between plant and animal food sources, which, as you can now see, are usually a function of blood group. Be sure to know your children's blood type, as it may help with any dietary issues.

Energy Field Alignment

We are made of atoms, and atoms are energy. Energy cannot be created or destroyed, it can only be transferred, which begs the question of where our life-energy goes when we die. It isn't destroyed, so is it transferred to a new life? Is this the source of our consciousness or the form of a human soul? Does this explain the continual cloning of Genetypes? Our DNA came from the universe, so what memories were imprinted on it before our planet existed? Our inability to answer these questions is the beautiful void between the two halves of the human brain, the divide over which both science and spirituality should shrug and shake hands.

There are times in our lives where we feel "disconnected." Disconnected from *what*? Through the process of genetic mutation, The Energy Field has given humans an elusive and powerful feature we call "consciousness," and arguably the entire planet was given this power, too; consider how certain birds and bees use a form of telepathy to coordinate ultra-close proximity flight maneuvers, and how flora communicate with each other through so-called "volatile organic compounds." So, by deduction, consciousness must be contained in our genetic code.

Consciousness is not only the key for developing your true self, your higher self, but it also is the key for taking control of your health. Studies have shown that by controlling your mind through consciousness, you are able to prevent stress, disease, and premature death and even able to reverse or eliminate damage and disease already affecting your body. In his book *Becoming Supernatural*, Dr. Joe Dispenza explains how the way you think affects your neurological, biological, chemical, and even genetic makeup. His research in neuroscience, epigenetics, psychoneuroimmunology, neurocardiology, electromagnetism, and quantum physics verify the correlations of health and consciousness and how you can defend or heal your body by transforming your mind.

Feng Shui, originating from the Chinese *Book of Burial*, is the art of optimizing The Energy Field for harmony, and architects and residents alike consciously or unconsciously aim to make energy flow through the building. Feng Shui even takes it as far as the location of buildings, aligning with water, weather patterns, and star constellations. To the frustration of many a realtor, even though a certain house may tick all the clients' boxes, the client may still say, "No. The energy just doesn't feel right." I doubt such clients are referring to Wi-Fi strength.

We also must agree that sometimes humans sense a certain energy about another human and that we can each give off good and bad energy, depending on our mood, allowing another human the possibility of reading our minds, to an extent. Would it be such a stretch to believe that there exists a similar kind of invisible "power grid" that flows all around us, perpetually available to flow *through* us if we allow it to?

My airline training exposed me at a deep level to scientific subjects such as aerodynamics, mechanics, meteorology, and electrics, and something that surprised me was how much of accepted science was actually a theory. For example, we don't know why it rains; we merely have accepted theories such as coalescence. We flick on a light switch, and a bulb illuminates, so nobody can deny that electricity is a fact, but it is a theory about precisely *why* this happens.

You really have to endure an advanced class on electrics to appreciate what a complex leap of faith electrical theory is; in fact, the day I stopped trying to *understand* electrical theory and accepted it on *faith* was the day I excelled in that class. In short, even science sometimes implies we have to accept something we witness based on faith, and that it happens to match the evidence. Imagine our world back when the only source of light we knew of was either the sun or fire, and then some guy comes along and explains that there is this invisible energy that can generate light. Incredulous, people ask him to prove it, so he flicks a switch and a light bulb illuminates, so we accept his *theory*. I now ask you to accept a theory that there is a spiritual light that illuminates the bulb in your being by connecting to The Energy Field that surrounds us.

Let's now take a practical excursion with a shortcut I designed to access The Energy Field. It must start with faith in the process, so slap some duct tape over your lower self's judgmental mouth. Even if you remain skeptical, from a scientific point of view, you cannot prove or disprove something until you have a clean experiment, so do not let ego contaminate your investigation. Faith leads to illumination, and illumination leads to certainty.

Now, situate yourself in a calm and peaceful environment, away from noise and distractions, at bedtime if need be. With practice you'll be able to do this with more and more distraction, but begin with the most accommodative environment possible. Once seated comfortably, close your eyes and vividly picture yourself in this setting you're in, as if you were on the ceiling looking down on yourself and what you're doing *at this present moment,* as if filming yourself with your eyes right now, a constant stream. You're literally engineering an out-of-body experience. Practice this until an involuntary smile crosses your face. You may also have a sense of melting or floating. You'll feel connected to The Energy Field. Don't fight it or try to rationalize or control it; let it flow through you for as long as possible or practical. Once we are aware of an inner consciousness, presence is not far away. People can even feel a part of them escaping. Tibetan monks harness this power and can melt snow in a circle around them from the energy escaping. This is a starting point of a much bigger philosophy that I can cover no more in this book, but I trust you felt the force of The Energy Field flow through you as you entered that abstract dimension discussed in the previous part of the book: *love*.

Foraging for Truth

So, apart from appreciating those previous three principles, what else can a time-traveling forager do to survive in modern society? In our unconscious and primitive efforts to avoid pain and seek pleasure in a time and place where "food" is abundant, we forever scout for a magic bullet diet. "No, trust me, this time I've really found the one. This one truly works! Yes, I know I said that other diet works, but this is it." Like startled shoals of fish, we flit from one diet plan to the next in an attempt to keep up with a tribe.

What if all the diet books are wrong? What if all the diet books are *right*? Diet fads come and go, leaving quarrelling "tribes" in their wake because most of the diets *do* actually work to a varying extent, *and that's because they virtually all overlap in key areas*. But, to distinguish themselves from other products, it behooves them to introduce a new set of "rules": don't eat this, do eat that, have as much as you like of those, often citing new research and/or some newfound chemical produced by certain foods that could be harmful. This process will continue for as long as we seek the magic bullet. I wouldn't take issue with it, only the esoteric group that The Diet Wars appeal to are not the majority of the population, and the average family is left simply scratching their heads in the face of all the fighting, freezing up from confusion, and resultantly not changing even the most basically harmful lifestyle habits. Thankfully for me, my mandate here is simply to keep you from harm, not to compete in The Diet Wars, and virtually all the diet books have a common denominator they all agree on: what *not* to eat.

The 80/20 Rule in action: *Stay away from processed foods, and avoid added sugars.* If you do nothing else, this common denominator that even The Dietary Dictators cannot disagree with will keep you safe. The catch is that, in this modern culture, it doesn't leave you with many options in the grocery store unless you home in on organic food that you can recognize back to its source. For example, if you want sweet potato, buy a sweet potato, not a prepackaged sweet potato casserole, and it will also taste better. Don't Open Processed Eats, and Added Sugar Sucks, or remember: "D.O.P.E.A.S.S." For the more mature readers, an update on the latest urban vernacular: "dopeass" means cool, not stupid or anything to do with cannabis. Having the word "ass" in the title also aligns with the current trend for featuring profanity in book titles. Here are a few more pointers for DopeAss living.

I begin each day with a well-researched smoothie that I've perfected over time and features the kind of healing roots ancients would forage for. I list the ingredients at www.JamesSheridan.com/recipes.

Meat and fish should be served in small quantities and from the most natural sources available (no pork, for if we are what we eat, then the same applies to pigs who eat their own feces even when free roaming on the pasture). Our ancestors often risked their lives to find these proteins, so they were not served liberally, so consider this the next time you see a 24-oz. steak on the menu! Our ancestors would also honor the animal and give thanks for its sacrifice, appreciating that we are all part of The Energy Field and a symbiotic ecosystem. What kind of energy must be in animals that are treated by modern humans in such a way as we do today? Forcing antibiotics and processed feed into them, penning them into compartments not much bigger than the animal—without exercise to ensure more tender meat—and then slaughtering them en masse by machines. I don't expect you to pray before the meat counter at the grocery store (you'd get some strange looks); just be discerning about what you buy there, ensuring the meat is from free-roaming animals raised on a natural diet. Yes, *certain* meat can be bad for you; but there is meat and there is meat. And there is portion control.

Critics of aligning our diet with what our bodies have been used to for the last 2.5 million years might argue that the average life expectancy of ancient humans wasn't far greater than forty years old. That argument is inherently flawed because it's talking about an *average*. High infant mortality rates in ancient humans, due to harsh living conditions and food scarcity, grossly skew the average age lower. If an ancient infant survived those dangerous first few years, average life expectancy is now shown to be far closer to what we're used to today.

I respect animal activists for campaigning against how we treat animals, and I respect food manufacturers that provide the more natural approach, but it gets complicated when we mix politics with nutrition. Proteins can certainly be found in a vegetarian diet, but if we don't consume any meat or fish, it becomes more work to get the essential proteins, healthy fats, and B Vitamins we need. Often this omission in diet forces people into *processed* soy products, which are therefore not DopeAss (or O-type friendly), however natural, simply because we can't trace soy sausages et al. back to the source; the natural source would be a soybean. Regarding getting your B Vitamins if you cut out animal products, there are supplements to compensate, but there are also two foods I'll mention here. In Britain, children are raised on a black goo that is spread on toast, called Marmite (or Vegemite in Australia). For entertainment over the years, I invited my American friends to try Marmite on toast, expecting the same reaction most times: they spit it out, gagging, and then exclaim, "It tastes like ass!" I like it, but if you find Marmite tastes like "ass," try *non-fortified* yeast flakes, readily available in grocery stores; they make a tasty, savory topping on almost anything and are bursting with B Vitamins.

Also, you must *vary* your diet as much as possible. One of the big secrets of our ancient forager ancestors was their highly varied diet due to their nomadic ways. For example, eat nuts and berries, but vary the type from day to day.

Get a DNA scan to discover any weak points in your genes, but don't think that your fate is sealed by it; it just means we have things to work on. Get a full blood panel test from your doctor, which will also highlight any issues, hopefully a good while before they become problems; the more you're ahead of the danger, the better. Whatever conditions you have or are in danger of having, there is usually a natural supplement for it, and when it comes to supplements, you get what you pay for. Do your research, and choose brands that use processes that don't destroy the nutrients with heat and pressure, and that have maximum absorption. Supplements are also often available as tinctures to add to drinks and smoothies.

Finally, we can't expect to be 100% compliant to any plan, and I enjoy an artificial licorice twist as much as anyone, but it's about understanding *the degree and frequency* to which we stray from such a plan. Ninety-five percent compliance? Yes.

The Solution Is the Problem

An ounce of prevention is worth more than a pound of cure, but a pound of what? We must focus on a cure of the *cause* not the *symptom*, but a change in diet may be too little, too late for many.

What killed the invading Martians in H. G. Wells's classic *The War of the Worlds* through "the toll of a billion deaths" were the natural germs that humans had earned their immunity from. I wonder if we are continuing to win this right when we consider the overuse of antibiotics in the name of profit. When a species becomes too interbred and does not give The Energy Field a constant diverse variety of new and improved genes to choose from, perhaps from geographical or cultural isolation, nationalism—closed borders, restricted international travel and trade—*or unnecessary use of antibiotics*, the result is "genetic drift," and the species becomes vulnerable to extinction. Genetic diversity is the challenge for any future colonization project, which is why Hitler's plan for racial purification was intrinsically flawed, but the Roman Empire approach of integrating conquered nations was not. *Diseases* from invading Europeans were the biggest cause of Native American deaths, not battle, due to the American content being geographically separated for so long (after the great migration) from a long intermingled Eurasian gene pool, hence with more diverse immunity.

Fortunately, our ancestors knew how to cure sicknesses; but we stopped listening to them after the advent of the same miracle that helped double life expectancy as we entered the 1900s: penicillin. Conventional medicine scorned the natural cures of our matriarchal past, when what it had actually done is hijack the work of ancient Egyptian physicians. Penicillin is basically mold, and mold was used as a natural cure in ancient Egypt for life-and-death scenarios, unlike the overuse of antibiotics we witness today for the weakest bacteria, and also viruses even though we know antibiotics are ineffective against them.

Drugs address symptoms, not causes, and they have side effects that offer a whole set of new problems that are potentially worse than the condition the drug is supposedly treating. (If you ever feel the need for dark comedy, watch a drugs commercial with the subtitles on and the volume muted, and read all the possible side effects.) "They" tell us all this is safe and not to worry, but "they" also once told us that cigarettes were safe (even good for us), and now "they" will still say that what we eat has nothing to do with our health. "They" have a different agenda to ours.

Some scientists will disagree with natural cures (lest their corporate sponsors pull their research budgets) or simply aren't taught them, but, ironically, science harbors the greatest proof of natural means to cure disease: *The Placebo Effect*. Any honest drug trial takes a willing group of human guinea pigs and divides them in half. One half gets the drug being tested and the other half gets a worthless sugar pill called a "placebo." The test is blind, meaning nobody knows who is getting the real pill or the placebo. By implication, science is saying that humans possess a psychosomatic ability *to heal themselves with mere thought* (by unconsciously connecting with The Energy Field) because of a sense of comfort. If simple thought can heal, so can the nutrients in your blood vessels, Vitamin C alone being one such nutrient that nobody will dare deny. Nature cures, but that's bad for The Establishment, which is something I learned the hard way.

In 2002, thanks to my business and investments taking off, I retired early from my career as airline captain and moved to America from the UK. Not long after arrival in my new land, I noticed an article in a mainstream British newspaper—*The Daily Mail*—that read: "How a collagen pill cures arthritis!" This was my first experience with how a natural substance was evidently able to do what a synthetic drug could not. I researched more and even discovered clinical trials that proved a certain type of collagen processed a certain way did indeed cure arthritis. So I found a USA supplier and secured a license to sell an appropriate supplement into the UK as an arthritis cure. Within the same week of the promotion launching, local government authorities shut down my UK operation because I had claimed that the supplement cured arthritis and I was not allowed to do so, *no matter if it was the proven truth.* This piqued my interest: "lobbied" governments acting as a police force to protect pharmaceutical company profits.

My reaction was not to slope away in shame as they would have wished, but rather to fight back in disgust against The Establishment, and the result was writing a fact-based novel that exposed one of the greatest natural cure cover-ups of all time. The 2007 book was called *The Pandora Prescription.* It became an international best seller that was published in four languages, but at the time of the book being published in 2007, many people also saw me as a conspiracy crank. Today, however, I see a growing movement for the kind of natural diet that *The Pandora Prescription* advocated, as more people are reversing diseases and throwing their drugs in the trash simply because of eating fruit and vegetables and giving up processed foods. (*The Pandora Prescription* e-book was rereleased in June 2020).

From The Dark Ages and the bloody Medieval Period that followed it, The Renaissance was born, and discovery of The New World incentivized an era of maritime exploration. British people earned the nickname of "limeys" from one of the big secrets behind the former dominance of The British Empire: her sailors could prevail at sea for longer because it became standard procedure for Royal Navy vessels to carry citrus fruits (such as limes) on board once they realized Vitamin C was the cure for scurvy, or almost anything that required immunity boosting. The British Empire holds the record for the largest empire in history partly because of a simple natural cure for an overwhelmed immune system, because her vessels contained real fruit.

Soon after the British invented something called a "corporation" to offer limited liability to investors in maritime ventures, the Renaissance period was interrupted by a revolution that would succeed thousands of years of our agrarian past: The Industrial Age. And with it came the temptation to worship a new god: money.

As you emerge from the information jungle that is health, a City of Gold stands before you, but you will need to know the pass codes to enter its gates.

part six

ADVENTURE
CAPITAL

A Hundred What?

On a hundred-dollar bill, does Benjamin Franklin look at us with disdain, or is it my imagination? It's as if he's saying, "I suppose you're going to blow this on a bunch of crap instead of saving it." Use cash instead of cards so the expenditure seems more tangible and painful, and this way Bennie gives you that look every time you whip one of his crisp bills out. But there's a lot more to prosperity than simply being frugal, because there is a limit to how much money you can save but no limit to how much you can make, only the limit you set yourself. And you must set one because prosperity merely facilitates purpose.

Any life map cannot ignore finances, especially if financial security and/or alternative income streams are required for you to live according to your purpose. Genetypes come into play in some financial matters more than others, to a potentially revolutionary degree in business, but in all cases it's what's hidden in *all* our ancient genes that allows you mastery of money. The final leg of any journey is traditionally the toughest, but this shall be the exception because the financial constructs of The System are merely a projection of human psychology, a projection you're about to see through. The freedom money provides might make it the biggest obstacle between you and living your purpose, depending on your Genetype, your current financial commitments, and/or how much sacrifice you and those who depend on you could manage, so this is an important step, no matter your Genetype and chosen purpose.

Two questions you might now have: How, when money didn't exist for the majority of human existence, can our ancient past help us with finances? How can such a wide and complex subject be mastered in a single part of this book? My answer is the same to both questions: It's precisely *because* human nature is so enslaved to our ancient genes that I can accomplish this, and I've spent the last thirty years of my life walking this talk as I perfected certain systems, symbols, and commonalities that capitalize on links to our ancient past. To master this final task we need to peek behind the curtain again to become conscious of our ancient instincts and *observers* of other people's. So let's take this in simple and chronological steps, once again employing The 80/20 Rule to get 80% of the benefit from only 20% of the effort required.

Money has existed for approximately just 0.2% of human existence; humans have walked the planet for two and half million years, and the first currency—the Mesopotamian shekel—appeared around 5,000 years ago. From a genetic inertia standpoint, money is a brand-new concept, but we know that it allows us food and shelter, so we rapidly adopted the basic idea of it.

Not long after money was born, it started being associated with evil, society ignoring the fact that when it comes to personal gain, the temptation for wrongdoing always exists. The idea of money being "the root of all evil" took hold. The Bible actually says that *love* of money is the root of all evil, not money in itself, which makes that a conveniently misunderstood verse. Before the world of *leveraged credit* we all now take for granted, where a bank can magically turn one dollar into ten, someone who had a lot of money outside royalty could rightfully have been viewed as suspicious or "evil." Before the invention of leveraged credit, if someone made a shekel, it meant someone had *lost* a shekel. So this idea of money being "evil" is outdated by around 500 years.

Money is now pieces of paper scribbled on by governments that say it can be used as legal tender for goods and services (although they back it with nothing of value). So the entire global financial system depends on trust in governments. This trust is rarely warranted. The problem is the corrupt governments that bastardize it with cronyism and money-printing to buy votes, usually abandoning an Old World "value anchor," like gold or silver, in the process. These policies we see today—"Quantitative Easing" and its successor under a new name: "Modern Monetary Theory"—are nothing new. It happened in the 1930s, and governments have a long history of debasing the money supply to buy votes and wars.

There's nothing modern about "Modern Monetary Theory," and (Quantitative) "Easing" wouldn't be my first-choice verb for an action that creates new bubbles when old bubbles burst. Both titles are politically palatable ways of saying the same thing: legalized counterfeiting at the people's expense, something even one of the most famous economists of all time—John Maynard Keynes— openly stated, albeit in a politer fashion. This is the reason why the average family's lifestyle has stagnated for so long despite them working harder, but in this part you will turn the tables on this corrupt system, at least until it is replaced by something honest. A currency that isn't backed by something tangible like gold is referred to as a "fiat" currency, and no fiat currency in history has *ever* survived. Ominous, then, that we've been on a fiat currency system since President Nixon declared as much in 1971, and unsurprising that we now see Federal Reserve policies grow evermore circus-like with each tick of the time bomb.

Let's start by working with the hand you have. It's what we can buy or do with money that matters, and if our common goal is happiness, the only true worth of money can be measured in units of genuine and lasting happiness it affords us (designer watches et al. do not provide genuine and lasting happiness). This initial revelation may seem obvious, but it eludes most people.

Because money is such a relatively new and abstract idea for our ancient genes, we struggle with an important question we must first ask ourselves: *How much* money do I need? Ask the majority of people this question, and you'll get a blank look, perhaps followed up by a round number such as "a million dollars." *How can you expect to reach a financial goal if you don't know where the goalposts are?*

Another concept we struggle with, also perhaps as a result of genetic inertia and our much simpler ancient existence, is the future tense. We assume tomorrow will be like today because for most of our existence *it was*. And this means we struggle to plan ahead. We must rectify this situation of having vague or nonexistent financial goals before we do anything else.

A to B

Our first step is to define your financial goalpost—a future-tense concept—and figure how much is enough before you have the financial security to live your purpose without concern.

The trick is to not succumb to fear and intimidation, to not make mountains out of molehills, but to *make molehills out of mountains*. In other words, to break the big goal down into little bite-sized goals, and then one day you wake up and you're there. Baby steps, day by day, and every journey begins with a single step.

The supercomputer between your ears blinks at idle with vague command inputs like, "I want more money." Your brain needs two data feeds to fly you to your goal on autopilot: *specificity* and *attainability*. The advantage *you* now have is that you not only have a very *specific* life goal (living your purpose), but it's also a goal that appeals to your true self, your soul, thus you are *automatically driven* to reach it. All that remains is the *attainability* part, and that's a simple matter of turning mountains into molehills. The command to the brain must be attainable in the immediate sense, not the abstract sense—the today, not the tomorrow. The future tense is a complication or even an omission to languages, our ancestors often too busy fighting to stay alive today to consider tomorrow, and evidently this legacy lingers.

It's remarkably simple when we break it down. You're currently at Point A, and you'd like to get to Point B. No journey can be navigated without this childlike concept, yet most people who want to get somewhere in life don't even know where *Point A* is. You now know your approximate Point B (whatever it takes financially to be able to live life according to your chosen purpose), and you must now figure out your Point A.

Figure your Point A in terms of its relationship to your Point B. What has to happen to get from one place to the other, broken down into the smallest steps imaginable? Every person who is involved, every transaction needed, every phone call that must be made, etc. Don't let the creation of this long list scare you. There is no immediate need to give up the day job if so required by your purpose; that may be the final task on the list and/or this could all be part of a sideline job or an escape tunnel that you'll learn more about shortly.

Next, *prioritize* these tasks in a 1, 2, 3 format for a logical chronology of events that take you from Point A to Point B. Think of it as a checklist.

Next, divide all these small tasks over however many days they need to be accomplished, making sure you're not being too ambitious or lazy in the allocation, and plot the whole thing in a calendar. I prefer a paper, week-to-view calendar, but use whatever works for you. Allow for breaks and weekends. For now, assume money isn't a factor.

It doesn't matter how far into the future this plot of tasks takes you, but once you see that date of the last task being completed, *carve it into stone.* That is your deadline, and it must *not* be violated. A goal is not a goal without a deadline, or it will mysteriously never happen. You may shuffle the tasks around in any given week, making up for losses, but you don't have a weekend until the tasks for the week are complete. *If* you've chosen your purpose wisely, this will not be a problem; it will be a pleasure.

Finally, and here's where the rubber hits the road, *complete every task in that calendar plot, every day, as if your life depended on it* (because it does). These are only small tasks, but do not let their apparent triviality deter you from completion or get distracted by the next goals on the list or the ultimate goal (future tense). This is breaking the mountain down into molehills, and *you must have rigid faith in the daily plan's completion ultimately leading to something greater.*

Whatever your purpose, you need money to live, the financial security to allow you to live your purpose until it yields an income (if at all), which is why we speak about this later. For now, from a purely financial point of view, your Point A is your current financial situation. If you're in consumer debt (as opposed to commercial debt on investment property, for example), it is a brake on your freedom and must be eliminated using the exact same process of breaking mountains into molehills with a day-by-day calendar, saving, paying it off, selling stuff you don't need (which by now I hope is a great deal), and to stop buying things you don't need, which is most things.

Once you have your financial Point A, you need to calculate your financial Point B. Figure out how much money you need to live each year, before tax. Once you have that number, you have your Point B. Based on that income you need, you can use the principles that follow to create it so that the income either flows automatically and/or is driven by your chosen purpose in life. Complete this exercise before moving on and you'll be in the minority of people who actually have a defined financial goalpost. *Your ancient instincts can now lock on to a visible target* instead of merely a vague idea.

Now that you have a definite financial goal, we must create your "mountains into molehills" daily planner. To do this you'll need to know exactly how you will get from your Point A to your Point B.

It's clarifying to know that there are only three legal and controllable paths to your Point B: real estate, business, and financial markets. As I mentioned earlier, do not be intimidated by these three subjects, because you're about to see how simple understanding our ancient past makes them.

As winter closes in each year, we have a custom of cheerily hanging a festive wreath on our doorways, not seeming to make the connection that it's the same wreath we somberly rest on coffins. Our ancient ancestors saw both rituals as a prayer because the meaning is the same: *Let the circle of life continue to turn. Let us survive through winter into spring. Let death beget birth.* One of our closest living relatives to our ancient past—The Native Americans—call it a "sacred hoop," and all our ancient ancestors accepted the cyclical nature of everything. The ancient Egyptians invented Pi—the basis of calculating a circle's area and circumference. The Mayan calendar was circular.

This human inclination toward *cycles* is locked in our ancient genes and is the key to mastering real estate, business, and financial markets on a macro scale. Until now, the hard part was knowing about cycles, identifying when you were in one, and recognizing what stage it was at. With cycles, ancient psychology, and Genetypes as the backdrop, let's now venture into the three financial paths that lead you from your financial Point A to your financial Point B.

Real Estate

What finer piece of "real estate" to begin this section on than The Great Pyramids? For reasons previously mentioned, ancient Egypt is our closest link to a far more ancient human past from 70,000 years ago in East Africa that shaped Genetypes.

The Ancient Egyptians were our most recent representatives of what's hiding in our genes, and they held certain numbers as sacred, particularly the number seven. Seven is a symbol of perfection and completion. Seven scorpions guarded the goddess Isis, the hieroglyphic symbol for water (a symbol for rebirth) has seven zigzag lines, the symbol for gold has seven spines, and *a legendary famine lasted seven years*—this mythology found its way into The Bible when it refers to seven years of feast and seven years of famine (Genesis 41:54).

We see the legacy in all religions today, and the power of the number seven is especially common. It is used hundreds of times in The Bible: fifty-four times in the book of revelation alone, where there are seven churches, seven angels to the seven churches, seven seals, seven trumpets, seven thunders, and the seven last plagues. The first resurrection of the dead takes place at the seventh trumpet, completing salvation for the Church. In Islam, the people turn around the Kaaba seven times, they run between Safa and Marwa seven times, they stone Lucifer seven times, there are seven commands, and seven sins. In Hinduism, seven is the symbolic representation of the world, there are seven "chakras" in the human body (based on our glandular system), and in Buddhism there are seven factors of awakening.

I could fill an entire book with the commonality of the number seven, but the message is loud and clear: *seven represents completion and perfection to all ancient cultures, as in a death and resurrection, as in a cycle completed.* Whether we simply made it up or whether this number actually does mean something isn't the point; the point is that its significance in relation to cycles has likely been imprinted on our DNA for all of our cognitive existence.

But what does the number seven have to do with real estate? There are a million different things you could talk about with real estate, but one thing is most important: *timing.* It doesn't matter how creative a "flipper" you are, how masterful a "lowballer" you are, or how cheap a mortgage you can get if you get caught out by a real estate crash like the one in 2008. At the very least, bad timing in real estate will hamper your progress toward your defined goal at Point B.

Now take a look at these years that follow, cast your mind back, and I think you'll agree that the times I write "Buy" or "Sell" next to them would have been advantageous to do so, in that you'd have sold at the peak and bought at the bottom of the cycles:

1966: BUY

1974: SELL

1982: BUY

1990: SELL

1998: BUY

2006: SELL

For example, selling property in 2006 would obviously have been an excellent idea because prices were at their highest, and the real estate crash of 2007–2009 was about to begin. You may also recognize that, unsurprisingly, throughout this historical sample, a recession wasn't far off once the real estate SELL signal was given, the most recent and severe being in 1991/2 and 2007/8.

Now count the number of years *in between* each BUY and SELL year (for example, 1967, 68, 69, 70, 71, 72, 73, in between the 1966 BUY and the 1974 SELL). It's *seven* years. You must become synchronized with this real estate cycle. If you do, you could make a lot of money. If not, your plans for having the freedom to live according to you purpose could suffer critical damage.

I realize this is hard to swallow. Whether something in The Energy Field is causing this pattern or it's merely a self-fulfilling prophecy that humans are causing isn't the point; the point is that this pattern is too defined to ignore and circles directly back to ancient texts and the symbolism of the number seven: the completion of a cycle.

As I write in 2020, according to this cycle, the BUY signal was in 2014 and the time to SELL should be 2022, but I have yet to see any real panic buying in this cycle. When I reflect back in time, the same was true before, though. The real estate market didn't really become frothy until 2005 despite the cycle beginning in 1998. The rate of price increase appears to be more exponential than linear, and ancient human behavior explains why.

There is a saying: "Every general is always fighting the last war." What typically happens is that the memory of the last real estate crash creates prejudice and caution in humans about repeating the mistake. This comes from our ancient instincts of learning from our mistakes and assuming that tomorrow will be the same as today. But people dramatically change this cautious view once they see prices rising and other "tribe members" making money from real estate, so the "keep up with the tribe (Joneses)" instinct takes over, and this then causes a bubble in prices as we swing to the other extreme (something we saw in "Generational Nurtures" in Part Two). This combination of ancient instincts in emotionally driven beings is the essence of hysterias and manias.

So, knowing about this real estate cycle means you simply stay on the right side of it, but that's easier said than done because we are emotional animals who instinctively want to conform and follow the herd. If you think back to 2006, dumping real estate at that time would've made you feel stupid and would've caused the rest of the "tribe" to ridicule you. And for a short while their laughter would've seemed justified because we can never time a peak exactly. As the 2007 real estate price "gulley" took hold, people justified it as a temporary blip on the way to higher prices. Denial is always a feature of the late stage of a cycle. Then, in 2008, people panicked to keep up with the "tribe" on the downside of the cycle, pushing down prices to the other extreme and sowing the seeds for the next BUY signal.

You have to ask yourself an important question both for real estate and financial markets: *Are you able to act independently of the herd mentality, the ancient instinct to do as the rest of the tribe does?* This isn't changing your nature; it's being conscious of it. Think about situations in life where you've done things purely because of peer pressure or because you said to yourself, "If everyone's doing it, then I should do it." Remember, the vast majority of people, sadly, are poor because they are unconsciously at the mercy of ancient programming that is betraying them in modern times. The majority of people buy when they should be selling, and they sell when they should be buying. The majority of people have no real wealth and simply live month to month. With that in mind, why would you worry about what *most people* are doing/saying/thinking?

Once you're synchronized with the cycle, you can start looking at the details of real estate such as rentals or flipping or commercial, etc. Bear in mind that we've now agreed that you must get from your financial Point A to your financial Point B, and this likely requires *capital gain*, not income. So buying real estate at a low price in the cycle and renting it out until you have a gain is one option, and the other way is to be more aggressive and active by constantly flipping real estate, the latter being a faster but more active path. Your Genetype will be best suited to one way or another.

You could use rental properties as a way to liberate yourself to purpose, but when you do the math with a conventional model you'll see a large Point B number. What do I mean by a "conventional model" for acquiring rental properties? I mean by using 20% or more as a deposit to get the mortgage. But if you can get away with putting less deposit down, your yield per dollar of rental will obviously go up, because it's all a matter of return on your money (i.e. the deposit you put down).

Even though I was flat broke after paying for my flight training in America, after returning to the UK, I made my first real estate deal when I was twenty-three, shortly after the 1990 SELL signal. Because of the economic climate I was able to acquire rental condos for *zero* deposit by asking the seller to pay my deposit for me in exchange for me paying full asking price. I used this method with two more properties. It doesn't hurt to ask, especially in the right circumstances, and when you put zero money into a deal, the return is infinite.

Flipping is the method of simply buying real estate for one price and selling it for a higher price after all costs, leaving two possible strategies: buying at well below market prices and/or *creating* added value with improvements. Each Genetype brings different strengths to the table, and you might consider forming a Genetypal real estate team on that basis, especially if it includes the more creative types who would see the potential in a fixer-upper or vacant land.

What about your personal residence? Home ownership is akin to "The American Dream." "America" was an idea before it became a country, an idea spawned by wealthy real estate owners, and that idea is a few hundred years old compared to millions of years of nomadic foraging tribal life. Is this "dream" in our ancient genes? No, and home ownership and the degree of home ownership satisfying our senses is Genetype dependent. At least FG-3/4/6 and MG-3/4/5/6 may have no such need or have lesser needs, and may wish to adjust their Point B accordingly. If timed correctly with the cycle, a personal residence will appreciate in value, yes, but you can only realize the capital gain if you sell it, and you'll be paying property tax on it in the meantime. So if owning a personal residence isn't important to your *true* self on your financial journey from A to B, better off allocating the funds to a more profitable project.

Apart from timing, we all know real estate success is about *location*, so here are a couple of tips about location. As discussed, humans are genetically nomadic in nature, perpetually migrating for one reason or another as we have done for millions of years. If we can figure out modern migration patterns, we can make early predictions about which areas are looking up in property prices and which are looking down. There are government statistics on this, but they aren't reliable or fast enough. And then there is your friendly U-Haul customer service rep and Starbucks barista. I shall explain.

Like any vehicle rental company, U-Haul rental prices can vary wildly depending on simple supply and demand. If you continually get quotes for a moving-size truck outbound from and to different cities, you can get a feel for the current migration patterns. For example, a recent quote from New York to Orlando, Florida, was over $3,000. The same truck from Orlando, Florida, to New York was around $700. That's instructive. Then, find the newest Starbucks in that up and coming area, and chances are you've found an area where prices are about to rise. U-Haul rates are truth, and Starbucks does their real estate homework well.

Business

Everything I offer in regard to business advice is done so in the hope that you will not cater to excessive or needless consumerism, and that you will be considerate to the global community and the environment. Doing the right thing as a priority will enrich your soul, not only your bank account.

Starting your own business shouldn't merely be seen as a means of getting you from your financial Point A to Point B. In fact, if you treat your business as a soulless and inconvenient means to an end, it will reflect negatively in the products or services you provide. Instead, your own business can and should be a *pure expression of Genetypal purpose*, and the resultant passion and enthusiasm will shine through to your customers.

Don't be scared off by not having a business degree. I've gingerly hired and reluctantly fired so many business MBA graduates that I've now lost count, because academia doesn't count for much in the trenches of the real world. Give me someone who is enthusiastic and hungry more than someone who sports an impressive resume. And don't worry about lack of experience because there are far more important things to worry about, as you shall see.

As French poet Charles Baudelaire said, "Genius is no more than childhood recaptured at will, childhood equipped now with man's physical means to express itself." That "childhood" Baudelaire spoke of is your true self before it became soiled by nurture, the plant under the rubble. So let us apply your newly acquired "Genetypal Genius" to business.

Business isn't rocket science because the core principle is already in your ancient genes. Trade as we know it didn't begin until around 3,000 B.C., and agricultural communities weren't formed until around 10,000 B.C., so business as we know it today is a relatively new idea to us. But the idea business is based on—the *risk-reward principle*—is fundamental to the existence of all animals, not only human animals.

Nature is efficient. Circles and spheres are the most efficient form of existence, hence why bubbles and the planet itself is a sphere. The perfect hexagons of a honeycomb are simply circles when you crush them together, for more efficient use of space. At a basic level, the risk-reward principle is about energy management. Organisms need energy to exist, but acquisition of energy requires exertion of energy, so it's a trade-off. In short, if you want to accumulate, you need to speculate.

To take a modern-day human illustration, you need to put gas in your car, but you'll burn gas to drive to the gas station. Gas prices at a gas station ten miles away are cheaper than the gas station one mile away, but it will cost you money to drive those extra nine miles. I'd like to think a human in this situation is weighing up the equation to ensure the extra drive is worth their time and money (although society seems so fixated purely on gas prices, I can't be sure). This may seem obvious to you, but when it comes to your own business, missing this basic point is one of the most common mistakes I see. Some self-employed people work harder and earn less than they would if they worked for someone else (which is fine if it's making you happy and wealth gain isn't the prime objective).

When animals hunt, humans included, they unconsciously and naturally apply the risk-reward principle. The reason why all animals instinctively attempt to keep up with the rest of the herd/tribe is because they're being watched by predators that are constantly making risk-reward assessments: the most amount of calorie gain for the least amount of calorie burn equals better net calorie gain, which means survival. So it makes sense for those predators to kill and eat the animal that is straggling behind, weak, or wounded, because it means *low risk for the reward*. Or, if you'd prefer a vegetarian edition, we instinctively pick the "low-hanging fruit."

The risk-reward principle is baked into our genetic cake; it's who we are. So why is capitalism so despised? This is a vital question you must answer before you embark on a business venture! If you're subconsciously harboring *nurtures* and prejudices that will insidiously betray your inherent risk-reward *nature*, you can expect a string of "mysteriously" failed enterprises. I'm not saying this from a scientific theory or business school standpoint, I'm saying it from the standpoint of twenty years on the front lines of the self-improvement industry and watching otherwise great entrepreneurs subconsciously sabotage their own goals and dreams. We must purge your system of this nurtured prejudice before we talk about starting a business, so please permit me a crucial sidebar.

Truth doesn't care about being popular or fashionable; it just is, so bear that in mind as I continue to tell it like it is. It's not that capitalism and the risk-reward principle are bad, it's that they've been corrupted by the very people we entrust to regulate them, so *the system isn't working for everyone.* Corporations can and will employ all legal methods to further their sole mission of profit. The flaw in the system is that a law doesn't exist that would throw a politician in jail for taking corporate funds or reward in kind, directly or indirectly, in any form whatsoever, and the lawmakers who would be threatened from such a law are hardly about to pass it. Politicians won't change, but they do need your vote, so let's next look in the mirror.

Think back to the previous part on health. Imagine receiving a letter in the mail from your retirement fund account manager who explains that your nest egg is worth 10% less because of the pharmaceutical stocks in your portfolio that have been adversely affected by smaller companies selling natural supplements. The manager then invites you to sign a petition to lobby against natural supplements and create laws that would prevent such products from making claims about their effectiveness, no matter how proven. What would you do? What if the town you live in is experiencing a drop in real estate values because the key employer of the area is a processed food manufacturer and is at risk of closing its doors because the population has turned to eating whole foods and cooking traditional meals? Would you back a bill to add a "special tax" on fruit and vegetables, or financially contribute to an "awareness" campaign that shows processed food to be harmless?

We all have an agenda, we all suffer from confirmation bias, and we are all part of the problem until we start thinking about the human race. We can't blame corporations for acting on their sole mandate, and perhaps we can't even blame politicians for protecting us (our vote) from financial loss. But we can blame ourselves for letting our own ignorance endanger our personal safety and financial goals.

When we learn that, in the face of rapidly growing and unprecedented adolescent type 2 diabetes, over 80% of public schools have deals with either Coca-Cola or Pepsi, we have no right to blame those two corporations for doing such a deal. How the executives of those two corporations sleep at night over this matter is neither in our control or our concern, *but their sleep will be nonexistent if we stop buying their products.* Aside from that, it's up to *government* to keep schoolchildren safe from the threat and to balance the corporate agenda, and to remember that soda corporations will argue that there *is* no threat. When we learn that certain ethnic groups are far more likely to be targeted for soda commercials than other ethnic groups, that isn't corporate racism; it's fundamental marketing. When those groups stop buying soda, the commercials will stop. When politicians ban advertising aimed at children, those commercials are *guaranteed* to stop. It's become unfashionable to ask people to take responsibility for their own actions, but I welcome an opposing view to argue with the simple logic I've just outlined, *ethics aside.*

A corporation is neither good nor evil; it simply *is*. The mission of any corporation is to make as much profit as possible through all legal means available, and it has a right to legally avoid tax. At any given time, the politicians are entitled to incentivize or penalize corporations to align with their own agenda of doing what is best for the *voters*. In short, all goes well in a free market economy when there is balance, reinvestment of profits, and private and public sectors that independently do their jobs. And there's the rub, or in the more eloquent words of Gilbert Chesterton: "The mere proposal to set the politician to watch the capitalist has been disturbed by the rather disconcerting discovery that they are both the same man." Capitalism isn't the enemy; government *cronyism is*.

There is far too much money to be made by corporations to simply walk away and shrug in the face of government interference in their mission, so they instead bribe politicians to further their goals. This isn't conspiracy talk; a conspiracy requires the act to be done in secret. This is all going on in broad daylight; but nobody is paying attention because cronyism is either indirect, covert, or termed as "lobbying." Lobbying perverts the course of democracy and capitalism.

Make all kinds of political lobbying or political insider trading or private/public sector career-mingling strictly illegal and punishable by long jail time, divert politicians away from corporate temptation and toward voter welfare, and we can all enjoy *true* and regulated capitalism. The only time to take pitchforks and torches to businesses is when they bribe (a.k.a. "lobby") politicians to get an unfair monopoly or preferential treatment, in order to gouge, defraud, or even kill the population. But that's not capitalism, it's effective *fascism*, by economic definition.

Thank God *that's* settled. But, judging by the latest whim of disturbing societal opinion as I write, it needed settling, especially if you have ambitions of business success. Now we can discuss the use of Genetypes in business.

The first objective is to activate your Genetypal Genius. Your passion must drive the venture, so ensure it aligns with your purpose—enthusiasm is contagious. Provided purpose is igniting fire in the belly, *all* Genetypes are capable of running a successful business, but some will have to work harder on certain areas than others. You may also elect to partner with other Genetypes who make up for any weakness you perceive in yours, and forging this kind of "dream team" alliance as the founders of a business can be extremely powerful and inspiring *if* they all share the core mission and values. They get "sweat equity" in the venture, and you get free services in exchange for giving them a piece of the pie.

To be profitable, the idea for your business must be more than simply your passion. Your passion is the driver and must link to the idea, but most of all the idea has to actually *solve what society perceives as a problem.* It doesn't need to be a brand-new invention or fill a gap in the market; the "low-hanging fruit" is actually in coming up with a new spin on something that's *already* filling a gap in the market, but it does need to solve a problem that may or may not be obvious to society.

Have faith that what you see as a useful product or service, others will too. Something I hope you take away from this book is an appreciation that you aren't alone in how you think and act. There are *millions* of people with your same Genetype, effective clones of you across the *world*, not only in your country; that much I know from firsthand experience of consultations and focus groups in various countries. Your Genetypal clones are invisible but every-where, and an ongoing project at Genetypes.com is to unite you with them.

One last point on business ideas, and it's a crucial one that our ancient genes and their struggle of future tense must deal with: the fast pace of technology. As I write in 2020, a little over a decade ago there was a pocket calculator industry. Then a single "app" on what would become standard on everyone's cell phone wiped it out. That was only the warm-up act. This isn't to scare you away from your own business. In fact, technology is opening low-risk doors for fresh entrepreneurs; you just need to put your idea through this filter before you test it on the market.

Technology is about to progress at a pace we won't believe, even by today's standards, as will the amount of disruptive technologies and business models. Even aside from destructive online business models you know such as Amazon and Uber ("back in my day" there used to be bookstores and taxis), robotics, biotech, and even cryptocurrencies will decimate entire industries. Robots are set to replace humans in up to a third of all jobs within a few decades. Wonder drugs from biotech are about to eradicate all known diseases, affecting drug and supplement industries and all the peripheral services that go with them, such as cancer treatment centers. And if you think cryptocurrencies are merely alternative payment systems like Bitcoin or Ripple, think again. Ethereum is a cryptocurrency with built-in contracts that will hurt law firms. Another crypto in development will effectively make car rental check-in staff redundant. This is only a drop in the tsunami of disruption that is coming, and your business idea must be able to stay afloat in it. If a robot could do it, if biotech could hurt it, or if a cryptocurrency could eradicate it, get back to the drawing board.

Working for someone is considered a low risk-reward scenario. Starting and running a business is considered a high risk-reward scenario. So the business school textbooks say. Technology and disruptive business models have turned this equation on its head. Having a job is becoming risky. Starting an online business, especially through a ready-made affiliate program, is not so risky.

If your idea passes all the aforementioned filters, it's time to test your idea on the market as cheaply as possible, and that means marketing. Genetypal profiling may or may not help you in your marketing, but if you truly can identify a specific Genetype or small group of Genetypes for your product or service, then you obviously have a distinct advantage because you can touch those people's emotions in a way nobody else could, because people buy things for emotional reasons.

Facebook and other social media has a "Customized Audiences" advertisement application that helps you select your target market, so if you have a clear idea about which Genetype(s) is your audience, you can advertise only to who your message is aimed at and tailor your advertising to them in a way never enjoyed before in history and in a more cost-effective way.

Online or offline, how will you *know* if your (Genetypal) marketing is working? Because you'll do something most businesses don't do: you'll track response. How many times do you hear businesses ask, "Where did you hear about us from?" or print a code on an order form that tells them where the lead or sale came from? Every dollar of your marketing spend must be accounted for and must pay its way, and online marketing gives you such metrics.

Next, your actual advertisements. Most ads you get exposed to are horrible, usually because the advertising agency in question cares more about getting awards than selling products for their clients. Next time you watch Super Bowl commercials, ask how many of them made you buy more of the product in question and how many were merely "clever" or "funny." The trouble is that our ill-suited ancient instincts, struggling for direction in an alien world, attempt to conform with what they perceive as tribal leaders, which, in this case, usually means Madison Avenue award-seekers. "Mad Men" will reasonably counterattack me with phrases such as "brand awareness," but when starting out you don't have the luxury of untraceable ad spend.

As a flashback to the part of this book on relationships, let's imagine you're an advertising agency and your potential client is Love, Inc. Love, Inc. isn't happy with its present advertisement for its "Couples Staying Together" product and needs it fixed. The executives at Love, Inc. explain that the headline on that poorly performing advertisement is: "You have to *work* at a relationship." Your task is to win the account. With our knowledge of the risk-reward principle and everything you now know about ancient human programming and how we instinctively want the low-hanging fruit, how could we improve this headline?

"You have to *work* at a relationship?" What a dreadful piece of copywriting. "Work?" The risk-reward principle indicates nobody wants to work at *anything*.

The classic mistake their advertisement made was focusing too much on the product (staying together) and not enough on the *benefits* of it; it focused on the calorie burn instead of the calorie gain. How about this headline instead:

Oneness is won.

I'll keep working on it, but the point is that I'm now subliminally dangling the *benefits* of staying together (oneness) without mentioning "work" or the lackluster idea of "staying together," while simultaneously throwing down the gauntlet by implying it's a *prize* because I have to *win* it. "Oneness" sounds somewhat abstract but seductive and sexual, making the reader want to learn more, which is all one can ask of a headline's limited real estate. "Truth well told," as copywriters say, not lies.

Are you buying it? Well, you need love and there are no alternative suppliers, so I guess Love, Inc. is a monopoly, which is why they can get away with such lousy headlines and flaky customer support. Or perhaps they have powerful "lobbyists." Your business won't enjoy such luxuries, so work on your advertising! The smallest things can make a massive difference. A copywriter dramatically changed the fortunes of one client with a *single letter*, altering their headline for a music course product from "Put Music in Your Life" to "Puts Music in Your Life." If you can spot the difference between those two headlines and figure out why it made such an improvement, you've learned the lesson about the risk-reward principle when it comes to marketing.

Genetypal awareness can benefit you in business in more ways than ideas and marketing. Everyone involved in the success of your business—customers, partners, investors, staff, landlords, bankers, vendors, etc.—is a human, *and that means they have a Genetype as well as an ego.* When you know a person's Genetype, you know which buttons to push to elicit a required response, so it pays to become intimate with all Genetypal profiles, not merely your own. (Once you know the sex, there are only seven to play an elimination game with.) This is "sniper motivation" as opposed to the customary, generic kind of motivation. You now possess the ability to speak directly to a person's soul.

Remember, Genetypes all have different priorities and dispositions, and it behooves the entrepreneur to get the best from all people affecting the business. Using Genetypes in human resources is a game-changer. Recruitment, motivation, training, even job allocation could dramatically make any business instantly more effective. Filling staff vacancies according to best-suited Genetype is a win-win, with the result of happier and more productive staff, less staff turnover, and more efficiency. Interview techniques also become revolutionized with Genetypal awareness, allowing the interviewer a way to quickly assess suitability of the candidate.

For salespeople and idea pitchers, Genetypal awareness is simply an unfair advantage. Use the customary small talk of any new encounter constructively by asking personal questions about that person. This will help you assess the person's Genetype as well as show you're genuinely interested in that person's life, making you likable to that person's ego. It will also help you avoid the people who might waste your time or money. The best entrepreneurs and salespeople already do this instinctively, but for everyone else, Genetypes provide a systemized way to do the same. And, incidentally, *systemized businesses are businesses that can run without you.* The overworked and underpaid self-employed example I mentioned previously would change their world with systemization. Systemization is also the path to franchising a business.

Once you've figured a person's Genetype, you know what's important to them and what fears they have, etc. This allows you to tailor your presentation for pitching ideas, getting loans, and most of all, selling. In a capitalist system, a government can't survive without taxes, and taxes don't happen unless people earn money to pay tax on, and nobody can earn money unless someone somewhere is selling something. Think about it. Selling is a lost art, so the competition isn't as strong as it used to be. Add Genetypal awareness to the mix and you have an even greater edge.

I often hear struggling realtors say things like, "A house sells itself." This is true to an extent, but a house also needs certain aspects of it highlighted to certain Genetypes, such as the safety features and school zones for children to an FG-1 (Nurturer) or an FG-7 (Matriarch), or an inspirational view from a *bed*room that could be better served as a great *study* for an FG-3 (Spiritual) or an MG-1/3 (Career/Creative), or the potential ability to build a larger closet for an FG-4/6 (Creative Femininity/Socialite) because you can see a cavity in the dry wall on the property plans. An MG-7 (Patriarch) would enjoy knowing that his property has the largest lot in the subdivision and/or how that subdivision is looking for a new HOA president (him). Potential buyers generally lack such vision or product knowledge, but a Genetype-aware salesperson merely needs common sense to do it for them.

There are a million things you *could* worry about in business but really only one thing you *should* worry about: *sales.* Who cares about how good the accounting software is or how accurate personnel records are if there's no revenue? You can always fix those things once you have sales. It's about focus and priority. It's about harnessing the risk-reward principle that's already in your genes, and it's about understanding Genetypes, especially your own.

Financial Markets

If real estate and business have no *obvious* meaning to your ancient genes, then financial markets take it to another level. Many people in the financial industry don't even understand them or the 2008 financial crisis wouldn't have become such an unforeseen train wreck. But markets appearing complicated is precisely what Wall Street wants you to think so you don't try to invest your own money. But there is hope because what you may suspect is the most complicated of the three paths to capital gain is actually the simplest *in terms of execution*. In fact, I will shortly tell you how to beat 70% of investment professionals in only four words.

When we discussed business, I explained that there a million things you could worry about but only one thing you should: sales. With financial markets there are a *billion* things you could worry about but only one thing you should: making a profit. It sounds simple, but in practice too many people forget what they're in it for; they feel they have to always be trading and analyzing and researching, but it all comes down to the ancient risk-reward principle once again: most amount of calorie gain for the least amount of calorie burn. As long as you're making a profit, who cares if you don't read *The Wall Street Journal* or if you don't listen to the dogmatic bull and bear "tribes" on TV? I haven't met many people who actually enjoy analyzing financial markets, but I've met plenty of people who want to make money.

The scramble for money is our contemporary game hunt, and financial markets *seem* to present a herd of bison backed against a cliff edge, but there are decisions to make. We could *guess* which way a buffalo will run and anticipate our spear throw, or we could *wait* to see which way it actually *does* run and then pursue it. The latter strategy gives the buffalo a head start, but it's less risky. This is the strategy I will explain now, not only because it's less risky, but because I have no telepathic link with bison.

I promised you four words that will allow you to beat 70% of investment professionals. It's from a single stock trade that you only have to make once in your lifetime, based on empirical evidence dated back to 1963. Here are those four words: "Buy the S+P 500." Then go to sleep for the rest of your life. You can buy as many shares as you like of "SPX"; that's the ticker symbol for the proxy investment vehicle for the S+P 500. The S+P 500 stock index has averaged around 6% a year, and *70% of investment professionals are proven to not do as well as The S+P 500*; that's to say, they don't even "beat the market." To paraphrase a famous saying, "If you can't beat it, join it," and evidently 70% of financial professionals should do precisely that.

When there's only a 50/50 chance of getting it wrong (buy or sell), why do humans evidently perform so badly in financial markets? Once again, the answer to the question is because we are unconscious time travelers, unwitting slaves to our ancient programming with our need to conform with a herd. Also, our ego (false self) makes us believe that we are always right and must not ever admit we are wrong. This is a deadly combination when humans play with the fires of financial markets, but it also creates opportunities. This nurture/nature cocktail is what drives hysterias and financial manias, and markets swing between absolutes of absurd values because of it. But getting in the way of it (by betting against it) can be like standing in front of a runaway train, at least in the short term.

We have a tendency to believe that tomorrow will be like today because for over two million years *it was*, and this is what exacerbates financial bubbles. When the market is down, we are biased into thinking it will always be going down, and vice versa. Legendary trader and hedge fund manager George Soros openly explains that his big secret is what he calls "Reflexive Theory." In a nutshell, his system takes advantage of the kind of extreme trends I'm speaking of by betting against them, but it doesn't come without a lot of pain. His fund getting it wrong nearly brought down the global economy in 1998. I say, *better to go with the natural flow*, and so do many other legendary traders.

The most useful trading advice Soros can give you is about the deadly nurture/nature cocktail mentioned previously. When we are making financial decisions that are academic—the outcome of which doesn't affect us—we generally make better decisions. But when we have skin in the game, we become what Soros refers to as "thinking participants," meaning that we now suffer from confirmation bias and cannot think objectively anymore because our emotions of fear and greed are in the driving seat. The same applies to other situations such as being emotionally or intellectually invested in something; if we want something to be true, we only tend to consider the evidence to support our theory. As legendary trader Jesse Livermore once said: "Markets don't beat men; men beat themselves." We will continue to get it wrong unless we overcome our ancient programming with willpower (change our "spots") *or if we rigidly follow a proven system.*

So simply buy the S+P 500, and it should *average* 6% a year, based on previous performance, and you'd beat 70% of investment professionals. But what if you'd taken that advice in January 2008, just several months before the devastating stock market crash that wiped 50% off its value? You wouldn't have thought much of that system then because of the timing of your first use of it. If you suffer a 50% loss, you need a 100% gain just to get back to even!

So can we time the market so that we employ this simple S+P 500 tracking system without the worry of first using it on the dawn of financial Armageddon? Most financial professionals will say you cannot. Most financial professionals don't even beat the market. Let's ignore them. I showed you how to beat 70% of investment professionals with a single trade, and now your ancient ancestors will show you how to beat the remaining 30%.

The drawback with simply buying The S+P 500 and going to sleep is that you ride the roller coaster down as well as up. Over time you come out on top, but ultimately it's a game of Chutes and Ladders, and you're expected to roll with the punches.. But what if there was a way to play Chutes and Ladders, only without the chutes and twice as many ladders? I found such a way, and it's been proven for as far back as I can take it.

In the section on real estate, you saw how the number seven has somehow predicted a life cycle of birth, death, and rebirth, and how the ancient Egyptians revered this number. The same representation of a life cycle applies to stocks: the average length of a bull market is five years, and the average length of a bear market is two years, totaling seven to complete the life cycle. An average historical length of a cycle isn't accurate enough to use as a system that offers precise entry and exit signals, but we are on the right track with "sacred seven."

Numbers are a universal language and can be linked directly to creation itself, from the perfect geometry of the nautilus shell to the honeycomb of bees. If we were ever to encounter an extraterrestrial species, numbers would be our first attempt as a method of communication. Prime numbers are the source of creation of all other numbers, and arguably the key to the universe itself, and seven is a prime number that has been intrinsically linked to The Divine. Numbers obey laws that humans cannot change.

Fourth-century cleric Saint Augustine continued the understanding of the secret of seven and explained it was the source of creation. Ten is also commonly used as a symbol of perfection and completion of a cycle, and Saint Augustine claimed that ten went even further than The Universe in its divinity. He also noted that when 7 was added to The Holy Trinity (3) it equaled 10. Whether he was right or not, the numbers seven and ten are used throughout human history across the world and are symbols of completion of a cycle.

After a quarter of a century of trying to find a consistently reliable investment system that offered the most reward for the least risk, I decided to experiment with numbers, especially seven and ten, to accurately signal the birth and death of bull markets. The product of 7 and 10 is *70*, and I applied it to historical charts of The S+P 500 as far back as I could go with the tools available: to 1982. The result was an average gain of 12% a year, trading an average of only 0.6 times a year.

When you use a two-times version of (ticker symbol) SPX, such as (ticker symbol) SSO, the gains increase to 24% a year. (I know there are triple leveraged versions such as UPRO, but spread and liquidity can become issues with it.) If you aren't in the financial industry, you may not appreciate the significance of this 24% annual return, but readers who are familiar with the traditional annual returns of around 5% are now either calling me a liar or drooling. So how's it done?

A stock price chart isn't usually a random hash of scribble; it's a visual depiction of ancient human nature and the risk-reward principle in motion, and often it appears quite orderly in the right format, even to the uninitiated. Number patterns on stock price charts are nothing new. What was new for me was using the number seventy in them, specifically my application of the average price of the last *seventy* weeks, on a rolling basis (referred to as the seventy-week moving average), as opposed to the benchmark forty-week moving average most commonly used. In short, if the S+P 500 is below its seventy-week moving average price, you should not be in the market and should go to cash on the first Friday it closes below this average.

As one example of many for how well this has worked, this exit (go-to-cash) signal was given in December 2007, several volatile months before 50% was wiped from the stock market. Cash isn't an investment? Cash beat the market by 100% in 2008! But the financial services industry can't let you know that, and "cash" doesn't sound like a "clever" investment that justifies fees. The last buy signal was given in early November 2016, and then the sell signal was given in late October 2018, resulting in a gain of 44% (with the two-times SSO ticker) from just one trade in two years. A severe drop of almost 20% occurred shortly after the subsequent sell signal.

The criteria for how to *enter* this trade (buy SSO) needs a few more boxes ticked, two of which also involve the use of the seventy-week moving average. I'll explain that as well as how to set this all up for yourself in the free video at www.JamesSheridan.com/sacred7. It takes five minutes to set up and another five minutes each week to check on. Once set up, I encourage you to perform the same back test I made with this system dating back to 1982 so you can see the proof for yourself. No system is perfect, including this one, but remember the priority: to make a profit, specifically a profit that beats the market (otherwise I could simply park all the money in SPX and go to sleep).

Despite the data speaking for itself, some people (usually with agendas) will criticize such a system, typically complaining that it doesn't involve use of "fundamentals," that there's no economic expert forecast behind it, no sound prediction of the future (which seems like an oxymoron). First, let me quote the most quoted economic expert, John Maynard Keynes, for what even *he* said about economic experts: "Practical men, who believe themselves to be quite exempt from any intellectual influence, are usually the slaves of some defunct economist. Madmen in authority, who hear voices in the air, are distilling their frenzy from some academic scribbler of a few years back." Second, anything that any expert says, including the "Madmen" at the beloved Federal Reserve (which, by the way, isn't "Federal" and has no "reserves"), and therefore their influence on market participants, *is already shown in the chart we're watching*. It doesn't matter how much you *think* something is worth, any item is only worth what it's worth—the price on the tape. Price is reality.

Sure, the market is often fundamentally "wrong" to trend in a certain direction, but being right when the market is moving against you isn't profitable, and the market can stay "wrong" a lot longer than you can remain solvent. The idea is to play chutes (bear trends) and ladders (bull trends), only without the chutes. There is no "right" or "wrong" market, and there is no "right" or "wrong" system, there are only profitable markets and profitable systems. Humans drive markets, humans are emotional, and those emotions are simply in our ancient hardwiring. Let the ongoing debates rage on, but results are all that matters, not fortune-telling, "Fedspeak," and flashing lights. It's like arguing over whether to hunt with a spear or a bow; as long as the animal is dead, who cares?

One final strategy to bear in mind, more as a backdrop for shorter-term trades. It's from something our stellar-worshipping ancient ancestors knew intimately and took full advantage of: *lunar cycles*.

"Luna" is Latin for moon in The Divine sense. The word "lunatic" is derived from "luna" because of the effect lunar cycles have on animals. Market participants are human animals, so lunar cycles should have an effect on price movements. The lunar cycle affects a lot more than stock prices; it literally can drive us crazy, specifically the full moon. The gravitational pull of the moon is what causes ocean tides to rise and fall. Organisms can consist of up to 90% water (60% in humans), so it's hardly surprising that the lunar cycle affects us.

In nineteenth-century England, "guilty by reason of the full moon" was a legitimate legal defense. Animal hospital visits for cats increase 23% around the full moon, and 28% for dogs. Eighty-one percent of mental health professionals believe that lunar cycles affect human behaviors, according to a study by the University of New Orleans. According to a 2006 study by Ilia D. Dichev and Troy D. Janes published in the *Harvard Business Review*, the stock market does consistently show signs of ebbing and flowing according to the cycles of the moon. The study took place over thirty years and followed twenty-five stock exchanges, concluding that stock returns received consistently higher returns at specific points in the lunar cycle. My own back tests of recent years show an average of around a 70% success rate and an average gain of around 4% for each cycle.

According to numerous studies and stock analyses, stock costs decrease as the moon wanes and increase as the moon waxes, so the basic rule of lunar trading is to buy (be "bullish") after the new moon, and sell after the full moon. In some Egyptian temples the waxing moon is shown as an aggressive young *bull*, and the waning moon is shown as a timid ox (a *castrated* bull).

One more cycle to bear in mind is the sixteen-year cycle. For an *average* of sixteen years and from a big-picture view, markets rise, and for the next sixteen years markets go sideways. A "macro" or "secular" bull market existed from 1982 to 2000 (even with the 1987 crash), and from 2000 to 2016 the market didn't really go anywhere. Since 2016 the market has been floating upward regardless of "fundamentals," much to the frustration of the bears, because 2016 to approximately 2032 is the next secular bull market. Sixteen is 4 squared—a quaternity of quaternities, a cycle of cycles.

The more emotionally or egotistically inclined your Genetype is, the more at risk you are when trading financial markets, and the more you must stick to a rigid system of rules that involves low frequency of trades. The opposite is true for the more logically inclined your Genetype is; for example, MG-1 and FG-2 would typically make excellent traders. Additionally, the more your ego (false self) is in control, the more clairvoyant and omnipotent you think you are, the worse your trading will be because you'll never be able to admit you were wrong, and that's expensive. I've never met a successful trader who wasn't humble, and that's because they learned this the hard way; the market humbled them. I'm saving you that lesson both for trading and life.

Nobody (and no system) can call the exact top and the exact bottom of a market, and anybody who tells you otherwise is a liar. It's not about being right as much as making your loss as small as possible *if you're wrong*, and, if you're right, letting the profit roll up as long as possible until the trend is over. Manage the downside and let the upside take care of itself, and that's what a successful system like Sacred 70 accomplishes. The smartest traders don't claim to know the future. They aren't right all the time, nor will they ever claim to be. They're just adept at finding opportunities with $1 risks if they're wrong and $5 rewards if they're right, and any sane person will play that risk-reward ratio all day long. (As I explain at my financial trading events, with that particular risk-reward ratio of 1:5, using a worst case sample for ten trades, a win rate of only 50% *triples* the capital! Do the math for yourself.)

After all you've learned, you can see how almost everything is a function of our past. As long as humans have these ancient behaviors hidden in our ancient genes, driven by emotions of fear and greed and the risk-reward principle and always trying to follow a tribal majority, the same patterns will continue. The SEC (Securities and Exchange Commission) is the government body that regulates financial markets in the USA, and they insist on a common legal wording for anyone selling financial services or products: "Past performance is no guide to future performance." Are they joking?

––––––––––

The only difference between penthouse and pavement in The City of Gold is knowledge, and your penthouse is where you think your quest ends. But high above the city, as you stare out the window at the streets below and then back across the life map you traversed, something deep inside you makes you run out the door, into the elevator, and down onto the streets. As you dash for the exit gates of the city to retrace your journey, you feel a tugging beneath you. You stop to look down at what it is, and you see it's a child clinging to your side.

Agitated and incredulous, the child says, "Why are you going back? You already have meaning, purpose, love, health, and money. What more could you wish for?"

Hugging the child, you reply, "The same for all my brothers and sisters."

part seven

THE
US CODE

GENETYPES AND THEIR DOMINANT DRIVERS

FG-1	Compassion
FG-2	Victory
FG-3	Spirituality
FG-4	Creativity
FG-5	Protecting
FG-6	Healing
FG-7	Partnering
MG-1	Logic
MG-2	Knowledge
MG-3	Creativity
MG-4	Philosophy
MG-5	Freedom
MG-6	Protecting
MG-7	Power

Tick, Tock

Nature abhors a vacuum, but that's what we have, and we are running out of time to fill it. I gave society a slap in Part Three because I didn't want anything standing in the way of you finding purpose at a time while your ego was still prowling, but of course, society is made up of individuals like you and me and everyone else, a Global Tribe. But our Global Tribe is fragmented and confused, and it faces a unique and imminent challenge to its survival.

In Part Six you saw how the cyclical tendencies of humans affect events. In Part Two, in "Generational Nurtures," I explained how a "mysterious cycle of events in human history" that Roosevelt described wasn't that mysterious when you understood the repeating societal dynamics behind it, and that it revolves around an eighty-year cycle between cataclysmic events in history (listed again shortly). The last such event was World War II, which began in 1939 (1941 for American involvement). If this cycle continues to make a correct prediction, the next cataclysmic event is due sometime around 2020.

Dominoes are wobbling. We are uncannily making all the same mistakes we did in the last cycle, with both the economics and the repeating generational personality alignment once again setting the stage. We have limited time to wake up and get a grip, and covering our ears in case bad news hurts them isn't a sensible solution at this time; the sound of explosions would hurt them a great deal more.

Every democracy carries the seeds of its own potential destruction. In Part Three I explained how overconsumption = "boom and bust" cycle = economic depressions = trade wars = shooting wars.

Now that you've read Part Six on financial matters, we can slot the original culprits into the mix: *Governments buying votes* = *loose monetary policy* = *easy credit* = overconsumption = "boom and bust" cycle = economic depressions = trade wars = shooting wars. Benjamin Franklin's reference to America being a republic "if you can keep it" is probably the *true* reason why he has that disdainful look on his face on a hundred-dollar bill, because he suspected his face would be printed a few trillion times too many. We are desperately and indiscriminately pointing the finger of blame at anyone and anything instead of the true culprits: governments and their cronies. Wiping out all debt is the best chance we have for this looming cataclysm to end peacefully, and there is precedent for this solution in ancient history with the Babylonians' "Clean Slate" proclamations. Needless to say, banks and their powerful lobbyists wouldn't be huge fans of such an event.

When bubbles burst, people search for a scapegoat, which governments are happy to provide, lest they (rightfully) get blamed for the misery. This leads to polarized politics, each side calling the other "evil," gladly wishing death upon the other, even their own countrymen, and demagogues circle the scent of discontent. Sound familiar? We are tearing ourselves apart and blaming anyone we can over anything we can reach for, our Global Tribe is busy with infighting, and time appears to be running out.

War of the Roses 1449–1487

Spanish Armada Crisis 1569–1594

Glorious Revolution 1675–1689

American Revolution 1773–1789

American Civil War 1860–1865

World War II 1939–1945

The Great Depression didn't end because of Roosevelt's grand projects and The New Deal; *it ended because of mobilization for World War II,* a "total war" (in that it was definitive). During each cataclysmic climax of the eighty-year cycle, a chilling common denominator emerges: both sides use the most destructive weapons available to them at the time. The last "total" war ended with nuclear weapons, but a new "total" war could *begin* with them.

With no purpose and no unity, we (our lower selves) default to our most primal survival instinct: caring only about our own self-ish needs that only apply to our individual life spans. Hence, we vote for politicians who pander to our short-term selfish whims, and politicians deliver them with fiat currency because they're thinking the same myopic way as us. We are now at the peak of this cycle, and we are armed with new destructive technologies. Operating in a spiritual vacuum with no balance, our selfish ancient survival instinct could, ironically, lead to our extinction unless we wake up.

As we stretch our hands out to what we *perceive* as a more civilized existence, we become off balance, forsaking the hard-won wisdom of our ancestors. We've forgotten who we are and what we used to be. Where did we go wrong, and how can an entire global society quickly correct its course?

Caging a Lioness

You know your Genetype, but does The Global Tribe also have a blueprint that we could recover and embrace the same way you did, to acquire a life map for *us*? I've made continual references to ancient Egypt and argued how the Egyptians are the closest link to our stellar-worshipping past that existed 70,000 years ago in East Africa.

And I've mentioned how when Homo sapiens migrated out of this region they carried this stellar-religion with them, hence we see the same pyramids on different sides of the world and the same mythologies told across the world, albeit in different forms.

Giza Pyramid, Egypt

Pyramid of The Sun, Teotihuacan, Mexico

By the principle of genetic inertia, the further back we can trace this ancient religion, the more imprinted its message on the genes of today's world population, and the more we can understand who we truly are. The hot debate over when the pyramids were built isn't relevant for this purpose; all that matters is how far back we can trace this ancient stellar-religion; what was in our *collective* psyche tens of thousands of years ago that, hence, remains hidden in our genes?

The Lion Statue of Stadel   *The Egyptian Goddess, Sekhmet*

In a museum in the German town of Ulm lies a significant clue with a connection that appears to have been missed: a hand-carved figurine of a half lioness, half human that has been dated to around *40,000* years old. The carved statue was found close to the museum. *This statue has a strong resemblance to the powerful Egyptian goddess Sekhmet.* Half human, half lionesses/felines were prevalent in ancient Egyptian deities and architecture, the most well-known example being The Sphinx.

When you consider that the great migration of Homo sapiens began 70,000 years ago and that the location that lioness-human carving was found in is 2,800 miles from Cairo *on foot* (i.e. the slow migration could've taken thousands of years to get to Germany), this is yet more evidence that *our early migration across the planet began with a fully formed belief system in place.* In short, a "master" religion was founded by our "master" race *at least* 70,000 years ago in East Africa. This religion later inspired pyramid builders across the planet, its imagery and rituals continually imprinted on our

DNA for tens of thousands of years, making the ancient Egyptian religion what we might call our "genetic religion."

When a "muscle car" revs its engine, many people become sensually aroused, describing it as a "roar." Why does a "roar" touch our souls? Lions have long been seen as "The King of The Jungle" by humans, hence recognized as a symbol of power, and our genetic senses have been exposed to that "roar" or its meaning for millions of years in East Africa. In the lion community, the lionesses are the hunters and the lion stands proud, like more of a figurehead, a relationship reminiscent of the king and queen pieces in the game of chess. This is symbolic of the basis of the ancient Egyptian religion, what I will now refer to as our "genetic religion."

Understanding the truth about ancient Egypt is The Us Code; it tells us who we truly are deep down. Ancient Egyptian culture was about the constant struggle of maintaining a *balanced* order over a slip into chaos, a balance between forces of light and darkness, *not* the conquest of one over the other. The ancient Egyptians believed there was no other human life outside their territory, and survival was totally dependent on The Nile River, specifically "The Inundation," the annual flooding of its banks, bringing water and silt deposits rich in minerals for growing grain. The return of the half lioness, half human deity Sekhmet was associated with the return of The Inundation.

The source of The Inundation was believed to be an unvisited holy place called "The Nun" (pronounced "noon"). Today we refer to a holy woman as a "nun," and we say we're "inundated" when we feel overwhelmed at a certain point in *time*; in-*nun-dated*, or overwhelmed by a holy event at a certain point in time. Hungry people are riotous people, and everything depended on this flooding cycle. In short, they realized how dependent they were on cycles and the environment. Today, we are just as dependent on the environment, only it's not as obvious to us as it was to them, thus we are blinded to the peril. Even before agriculture came along, when we were East African foragers, there was a precious balance with, and respect for, the animal kingdom, their sacrifice always honored and measured, lest the herds not return. Understanding this precious balance and vulnerability is in our genes, our guts, but we aren't listening to it.

The most important aspect of balance in ancient Egyptian society was between The Masculine and The Feminine, particularly in the balance of their respective philosophies (that are reflected in the Genetypal Dominant Drivers). Our contemporary patriarchal, black-and-white mentality makes us scratch our heads and ask: so was it a patriarchal or matriarchal system?

Look closely at ancient statues of Egyptian kings and queens, and you'll notice that they sit side by side as equals, that the queen's arm is around *the king* (a sign of possession that we are accustomed to seeing vice versa today) and that the king wears a wig to match the queen's hair. Our genetic religion is a solidly matriarchal one; but today we don't understand what matriarchy truly means.

When you look at everything through a patriarchal lens, the lens of linearity and logic, you judge everything by that standard. Patriarchy is male dominance with females pushed down, but matriarchy is about *equal balance* between the two, *not* females as dominant. Matriarchy *is* balance and equality. With reference to matriarchy, the Egyptians were referring to an all-encompassing *philosophy of balance*, not the dominance of one sex over the other. This is something most contemporary males don't appreciate (because of patriarchal thinking), hence the dogmatic resistance to the idea of matriarchy and accusations of being "gay" or "weak" scoffed at any male who presents what *appears* to be a submission to female supremacy.

So, males don't often forward the idea of matriarchy, and even *females* often don't because they've learned that contemporary males find it unattractive, often leaving FG-5 (protector of the vulnerable) as the lone champion for the cause, with no reward other than being branded a "rabid feminist" or similar. This false image of what matriarchy represents must be shattered, because it's the polar opposite of what our genetic religion espouses, and for good reason.

The ancient Egyptians understood that *both* males and females brought different things to the table that were crucial to survival, and I'm not only talking about genitalia. The Masculine and The Feminine are independent philosophical principles. The right side of the brain and left side of the body is The Feminine, and the left side of the brain and right side of the body is The Masculine. The wedding band is on our left finger, and people with two left hands are prevalent on Egyptian carvings, indicating exclusive *giving* (the right hand was associated with taking, and the left with giving).

There is no reason why contemporary humans' brains should trigger a positive response when being kind or a negative one when being mean, other than this Feminine philosophy of kindness that was long imprinted on our DNA. Christ conquered Rome posthumously and peacefully because his core message was kindness. Imagine how much faster and far-reaching a unanimous message of kindness could go today with The Internet.

Egyptian carvings and hieroglyphics are littered with a symbol called the *ankh*. An *ankh* is a representation of a penis and a vagina, the loop atop the cross obviously representing the latter, and the whole symbol forming a quaternity, a cross, like so many symbols that represent a quarterly cycle such as the seasons or the menstrual cycle or the lunar cycle to name just a few. The *ankh* means *eternal life,* a regeneration of souls. As I explained in Part One, through your Genetype, you have been here before and shall be here again.

Ankh

The Masculine philosophy represents logic, rationality, dogma, ego, history, and *linear time.* The Feminine philosophy represents emotion, spirituality, eternity, altered states of consciousness, and *cyclical time.* We need both philosophies for a balanced society, but only one side allows us access to the spiritual. At the entrance

Snake and Vulture

to ancient Egyptian temples it is common to see an emblem of a snake and vulture. The snake represents The Masculine, and the vulture The Feminine.

A snake cannot fly, but a vulture can, the meaning being that for one to enter the temple, one must leave The Masculine behind and surrender to the spiritual (Feminine) side of yourself, or your *higher self*. Many national flags or logos incorporate birds or wings, but none make such a parallel to the snake and vulture concept as Mexico's, which is especially interesting when we recall that Mexico

and Egypt are the two countries with the largest pyramids and have similar latitudes, meaning similar stellar significance.

Today, males constantly whine about the "mysterious" ways of females, when it's simply that females don't fit into their logical, patriarchal box. *Nature* moves in mysterious ways, as the spiritual world of a female, and the ancients knew so. We insist on believing we are more intelligent than our ancient ancestors because we invented things like smart phones, but our ancient ancestors were around a lot longer than we have been or stand to be, at this rate.

Our genetic religion learned a hard lesson during tens of thousands of years of hard living, and it's buried deep in our contemporary gut, but we aren't listening to it: when The Masculine moves out of balance with The Feminine, when it rises above it to become patriarchal, it is the road to destruction. When we cut ourselves off from the spiritual, from nature, from our emotions, from our *higher selves*, society falls apart.

So, what happened when we took the wrong fork in the road? Evidently, the Homo sapiens who didn't get very far after the great migration—the ones who settled around The Mediterranean such as Greeks and Persians—lost their pure matriarchal religion and became belligerent, eventually turning on their mother civilization. Notice how the evidently more spiritually driven humans who went the distance on their sun-following quest and made it to Asia and then America mostly founded peaceful beliefs that appreciated balance and nature—the Buddhists and Native Americans, with the Yin and Yang symbol and "sacred hoop" beliefs.

Only as far back as 2,500 B.C. is where most conventional Egyptology focuses, and by then Egypt was steadily slipping into patriarchy, partly thanks to an elitist priesthood. This is why ancient Egyptian culture can mistakenly be seen as patriarchal and brutal—especially in biblical references—because of the recent time frame it's commonly seen in.

In 525 B.C., Persians invaded Egypt, executed the royal family, and shifted the balance further off. The Romans came next, monotheism took over Rome a few hundred years later, and the loop on the *ankh* was closed. A closed *ankh* was the inheritance of The Dark Ages that followed. And The Crusades came after that—the bloody signature of Medieval Times. The Renaissance was a glimmer of hope, the artistic side of The Feminine blossoming and booming, but it was interrupted by The Industrial Revolution a couple of hundred years ago, and here we are.

Our scientific accomplishments have been astonishing, particularly in the last hundred years, and they have made our lives safer and more comfortable, but there is no balance. As we gaze into our electronic tablets, dazzled and seduced by this window of entertainment and convenience, we are blinded to our ancient window to the spiritual, rendering our souls iNeffective.

But we didn't lose our genetic religion, because a few thousand years of patriarchy is only a few percent of our genetic memory imprints that span up to 70,000 years. It still exists within us. The ancients' matriarchal culture spoke to people in a subliminal way that infected their subconscious, in a certain code that would ensure their crucial message of Masculine and Feminine balance would long outlive them and be carried across the planet by their descendants, only to be understood by the deserving future generations of humanity. This code still lies dormant in our genes, in our unconscious, waiting for resurrection.

How so? When you look at the world only through the lens of logic, everything is black and white and two-dimensional. To understand the ancient message, you have to think like an ancient Egyptian: in the abstract. Grab some popcorn; we're going to the movies so I can explain. After all, we are *star* worshippers at heart.

Rescuing the Sky Goddess

"The best stories come out of truth." – Ridley Scott

"One of the things you do as a writer and as a filmmaker is grasp for resonant symbols and imagery without necessarily fully understanding it yourself." – Christopher Nolan

Shamans are alive and well today; they just don't know they're shamans, but they are consciously or unconsciously keeping our genetic religion alive. Certain people are particularly attuned to The Energy Field, it "speaks" to them with a "hidden hand," and they are the medium between the spiritual world (Feminine) and the material world (Masculine). The abstract is what speaks to the side of us that is devoid of ego, our false self, and instead speaks to our *true, higher* self. It's the difference between speaking literally and figuratively, also known as speaking metaphorically.

Metaphors are the language of the higher self, our *soul,* and this was the matriarchal language of the ancient Egyptians. This abstract language frustrates patriarchal, contemporary scholars who can't figure out why, for example, there are several Egyptian temples all named after the same goddess. Our unconscious mind is where our dreams and *déjà vu* come from, and where tens of thousands of years of memory imprints on our genes take hold. Metaphor was the code of the ancient Egyptians, and they embedded our genetic religion in our unconscious in this way, to preserve us.

Stories circumvent ego. The Masculine side of humanity, ego, is dogmatic and judgmental, so the ancient shaman would tell stories that resonated to The Feminine side of us, the spiritual, to touch souls and liberate beings from the clutches of ego. This is why Plato feared storytellers—because they possess the ability to influence the population in a potentially undesirable way without them realizing. Plato's fears came to pass the day we became a patriarchal society. These specific kinds of stories are known as *myths*, and ancient Egyptian myths are the original templates, their plotlines woven inside us to this day.

Today, one popular medium that shamans tell their stories through is film. People in the film industry have a saying: "Nobody knows what works." The shamans know, but perhaps they just don't know they know. When a particular key ancient myth is metaphorically encoded the right way in film and television, the work "mysteriously" takes off as the Global Tribe sings its praise in unity but can't explain why. It's not that *they* can't explain it, it's that their judgmental, ego-based, lower self can't. But deep down, the higher self and its ancient antenna has been awoken with a message from our genetic "master" religion, and the lower self is left picking up the pieces, confused.

The shaman's trick is in not waking up the sleeping dragon of ego, and to tiptoe around it to speak to the higher selves of the audience. This is something metaphorically explained head-on in Christopher Nolan's *Inception*, where the challenge of the heroes was to evade detection of the "projections" of the subject's mind they had infiltrated, or the dream would collapse.

A shaman has to suspend the audience's disbelief, send it into a trance, and the second it snaps out of that trance is when the story and the shaman lose their power. It's a form of hypnosis, even a form of exorcism if seen as rescuing one's soul (true self) from the fires of hell (ego). One technique is to keep the ego distracted with conflict or linear concepts that appeal to The Masculine, a tactic *Inception* masterfully pulls off to the audience *and* as a tactic used by the protagonist to achieve his mission. The *Inception* plotline is based around Cobb, a man who must make a *descent* through dream states to rescue his dead wife from his own guilt. As we are about to see, rescue of a matriarchal figure is significant, but not in the fairy tale sense, as discussed in Part Four. To the "snake," *Inception* is a scribble-scrabble of conflict, to the "vulture," it is a spiritual journey. *Inception* is a modern myth.

James Cameron's *Titanic* was a worldwide blockbuster that left swaths of people "inexplicably" singing the theme song for decades later. Why? We all knew how it would end! But when another studio attempted a "me too" movie in the form of *Pearl Harbor*, it didn't enjoy the same iconic success. Why? Surely the winning formula was "star-crossed lovers on a collision course with a famous historic tragedy?" No, it wasn't. Rose, *Titanic*'s female (FG-7 Matriarch) protagonist, is trapped by the epitome of patriarchy, but she is rescued by a man who speaks to her soul, parading her on the bow of the ship, worshiping her as a goddess as he rescues her and releases her into the wild. Although the FG-7 Matriarch Genetype is tough and defiant, the Matriarch cannot rescue herself, for she is in lockstep with a "king" to maintain the balance; it is up to others to liberate her.

Rose makes a *descent* into the belly of the ship, the "belly of the whale" and her inner self, to witness another, more spiritual side of life. Now, had Rose said, "Listen, mother, I'm going to make a descent within myself to find out who I am and what my purpose is," the audience would've groaned and walked out of the theater as Christopher Nolan's "projections" gunned down the metaphor and made the audience's dream collapse, because that is not the abstract language of The Feminine.

Before *Titanic*, James Cameron made more of a direct reference with *Aliens*, triggering a cult following that fueled the franchise in a way the previous film, *Alien*, had not. Another female protagonist, Ripley, who is straight-up FG-5 (Protector of the vulnerable), in the climax of the film, makes a *descent* in an elevator to rescue a child called *Newt*. The Egyptian Matriarch, the sky goddess "Nut," is pronounced the same way. Newt is a feisty and resilient (FG-7 Matriarch) child who clutches the decapitated head of a doll as a direct association with Nut's daughter, Isis, who lost her human head so she could become a goddess with an animal's head in Egyptian mythology.

The male characters in *Aliens* are mostly portrayed as materialistic, misogynistic, and violent slaves to science, not to bash males, but to highlight how far the balance is lost in this future world. *Aliens* is a direct reference to an FG-5 Protector rescuing an FG-7 Matriarch to restore harmony and balance to a patriarchal world. It's noteworthy that there is an *alien* queen that must be replaced by a *true* "queen"; female leaders sometimes don't ring true for us because we sense they are not true matriarchs but rather more like patriarchs in women's clothing.

In the final sequence of *Aliens*, after Ripley blasts the alien queen out the air lock, Newt is saved from the same fate by the android, and the two hug. Thanks to an FG-5 Protector, the science/logic philosophy of The Masculine has been brought into balance with The Feminine, and technology has become in service to humans, not humans in service to technology. This point was also made in Stanley Kubrick's sci-fi masterpiece *2001: A Space Odyssey*, when the ship's computer "HAL" was shut down in order for humans to see the next stage of their evolution and for the mission commander to be visibly *reborn*. Once HAL is deactivated, the screenplay suddenly and dramatically transforms from a linear ("snake") plot to an abstract ("vulture") plot. What became an iconic theme song for the film was "Thus Spoke Zarathustra," Strauss's 1896 musical tribute to the very same Nietzsche text referenced earlier in this book.

Ridley Scott directed *Prometheus* as the prequel to *Alien*. In *Prometheus*, Scott masterfully balances The Masculine with The Feminine—science with spirituality—throughout the film, as well as offering an explanation about where the first organism came from on earth. We learn that cave drawings point to our stellar-worshipping past. Later, we see that 2,000 years ago (note the timeline), the humanoid species we derive from tried to exterminate us because we switched religions. The female protagonist has an *immaculate conception* of sorts as the imagery continually flicks between life and death, birth and rebirth, the latter being the core theme of our genetic religion.

On the surface, *Downton Abbey* appears as merely a mildly interesting period drama, and yet it became a global phenomenon with people who've never drunk tea in their life suddenly having "afternoon tea" and attempting to speak the Queen's English while they're at it. Screenwriters are taught that conflict drives a story forward, but *Downton Abbey*'s story is driven forward by *kindness*. This is a masterfully executed screenwriting rule-breaker from Julian Fellowes, and it is the core message of our genetically imprinted master religion.

In Sam Mendes's *American Beauty*, a carefree MG-5 (Freedom) man is married to and totally compliant with a competitive FG-2 (Victory) woman, a Genetypal ticking time bomb that triggers when he is spiritually awoken by the sight of a young and flirtatious FG-4 (Creativity) cheerleader. Everyone is living a double life in this film, bouncing between lower self and higher self both materially and spiritually. Symbolic motifs of mirrors and cameras abound, the FG-2 (Victory) even slapping and screaming at herself as if another entity is inside her. Eventually, there are spiritual rebirths, with the MG-5 (Freedom) husband going with his true nature of

living a life with "the least amount of responsibility possible," and the FG-2 (Victory) wife having an affair with an MG-7 (Power) man.

When the male protagonist finally gets his fantasy of the young cheerleader sexually surrendering, he refrains from intercourse after learning she is a *virgin*; by instead covering her naked body and making her a sandwich, he chooses the higher fork in the road and resists the path of a mindless animal. His rebirth does not require another person to conceive it, it is an *immaculate conception* of his true self, and the virgin retains her virginity despite her "giving birth" to this man's awakening and new self. By the end, the husband and wife's spiritual rebirths give them compassion and commonality and the prospect of a revival of their marriage, but it is too late because the MG-7 (Power) neighbor was too afraid to awaken his higher self. And there's the rub: we *all* have to awaken for society to come back into balance.

Scott, Cameron, Nolan, Mendes, and their kin are mighty shamans indeed. For an example of a more expansive story template, none rivals George Lucas's *Star Wars*. My mother took me to see this film when it first stunned the world in 1977, and since then, it has become a global phenomenon that is unmatched, so I suspect there is more driving the popularity than special effects, sci-fi freaks, and fan boys.

Star Wars is one long struggle of a spiritual (Feminine) world attempting to balance with a material (Masculine) world. "The Force" is a direct reference to The Energy Field. The dark side of the force is The Masculine, ego, epitomized by fear and anger. Just as ancient Egyptians, Jedi expect both light and dark sides of the force to exist, but they must remain in balance ("balance" is a common word in the script). Anakin Skywalker's FG-1 (Nurturing) mother gave birth to him through an *immaculate conception*; The Force impregnated her. MG-7 (Power) Anakin is full of ego and a wild card, but his unity with FG-7 Matriarch, Padme, offers balance. Patriarchy rises above matriarchy when Anakin forsakes Padme, is consumed by ego, and becomes half machine (conquered by science) as a result. Their society, The Republic, crumbles, and *Paradise is lost.*

But there is a "new hope," a new birth, because Padme had twins called Luke and Leia. As an adult, it's notable that Luke begins as a farmer gazing at the horizon, as does the protagonist in Christopher Nolan's *Interstellar*, a reference to the explorers we once were before we became agrarian. Luke leads an unlikely band of characters in a secret mission to *rescue a princess*. MG-6 (Protector) Han Solo epitomizes the unchecked Masculine when out of balance: ego-tistical, selfish, belligerent, and cynical, and his solution to every problem is to "blast" it. As sci-fi shaman, MG-3 (Creativity) Obi Wan tells him, "There are other solutions to fighting."

Leia, a straight-up FG-7 (Matriarch), is the customary handful for that feisty Genetype and the proverbial "woman scorned" if crossed. When her ship is boarded, she kills storm troopers before squaring up to MG-7 Patriarch Darth Vader and giving him what for. She's not so much captured as silenced and discarded. Once Leia is *rescued* by Luke and Han Solo, the lioness is out of the cage, and she immediately asserts herself, banging the boys' heads together and saying, "Get this walking carpet out of the way." She's coming through. This woman has a galaxy to run, and amateur hour is over. She promptly puts The Masculine in its place by telling Han Solo, "If money is all you love, then that's what you'll receive." Rescuing the sky goddess shifts the balance. "Into the garbage chute, flyboy!"

From Luke switching off his "targeting computer" to a band of spiritual, forager-like creatures called Ewoks defeating The Empire without any technology, nature is eventually brought back in balance with science, and Feminine is balanced with Masculine.

Luke's journey to find his father is a classic metaphor for the search for one's true self. He eventually realizes that destroying MG-7 Patriarch Vader means destroying himself (the child of lower self at his side) as he compares his father's severed right hand (the hand of taking) to his own severed right hand. *Aggression will not bring the patriarch back to balance; love and compassion will.*

A dying Darth Vader says (emphasis his), "Take off my mask so I can see you with my *own* eyes." Luke lifts the mask from Vader, peeling away Vader (false self) to reveal the true self of Anakin Skywalker. Vader's "doors of perception" are suddenly cleansed, and he dies in order for Anakin to live on spiritually, a sacrificial death and then a spiritual resurrection. This is a *rebirth*.

And, united, The Global Tribe worshipped *Star Wars* for decades later and beyond, even officially forming a *Jedi* religion (Jediism), all thanks to a contemporary shaman, George Lucas, his one voice resonating with one sacred message hidden in our ancient genes. Perhaps we should pay attention.

Religious wars, mass murder "martyrdom," and associated frictions ignite from the stupidity or ignorance of not correctly interpreting the one basic metaphor from our common ancient ancestors. The function of a priest is supposed to be as *interpreter of the metaphor.*

When priests and people can't get beyond the one ancient metaphor, when we see differences instead of commonality, blood is shed on a biblical scale. Our priests used to be shamans.

We don't have to change who we are as a society; we simply have to awaken to what we *already* are, and compassion is our code. The more we have strayed from this code, the more destruction there has been. This is the inherent compassion of The Feminine, the spiritual side of us required for rebirth. But to accomplish this as a society we must rescue The Sky Goddess, the matriarch, bringing the philosophies of Feminine and Masculine back into balance.

Your purchase of this book means you've participated in a "rescue mission" because 20% of my profit from it goes to charities focused on women's shelters and defending against domestic violence. Thank you.

Say a Prayer

I have learned so much from God that I can no longer call myself a Christian, a Hindu, a Muslim, a Buddhist, a Jew.

The Truth has shared so much of itself with me that I can no longer call myself a man, a woman, an angel, or even pure Soul.

Love has befriended Hafiz so completely it has turned to ash and freed me of every concept and image my mind has ever known.

Hafiz, Persian poet (1315–1390 A.D.)

The pyramid represents four divided sides that become as one at the peak, unity when closest to God. Whatever your faith or spiritual inclination, whatever you may think of ancient peoples and philosophies, there is no denying we are all made of stars and that we all come from a Motherland in and around Egypt that fostered a religion centered around the principles of matriarchy. After tens of thousands of years of imprints on our DNA, *this is who we are.*

My statement about a universal "genetic religion" doesn't trounce faith; it liberates it, elevates it, unites all genres of it, and includes a path for those who are spiritual but don't require a church or temple to honor it. We all genetically believe in the same thing, and *something in our DNA gives us a need to worship something greater than ourselves*; we just have different ways of expressing it. People won't enter an ice cream shop if all they ever see inside is patrons fighting over what is the best flavor ice cream. We simply have to bond from the fact that we all like ice cream.

But what exactly is that same thing we all believe under the surface? Today, the prevailing patriarchal, hence literal and linear, thinking assumes that ancient Egyptians were obsessed with death. They weren't obsessed with death; they were obsessed with *rebirth.* Rebirth is the *cyclical time* of The Feminine, not the linear time of The Masculine. Death begets birth, much as you had a "second birth" at the end of Part Two when you found your Genetype. It was "a second coming."

Seventy thousand years ago we gazed at the sun and migrated across the planet. We believed The Sky Goddess, Nut, gave birth to the sun in the east and swallowed it up in the west. We saw sunrise as a rebirth to give thanks for, and we believed that each sunrise was a new beginning for the cosmos. Every day you see the sunrise *is* a new day, a new chance, and a time to be gracious for how special it is that we even exist on this miniscule rock in an unfathomably vast universe, a universe that retains a "mysterious" *balance* that defies Big Bang Theory.

Your ancient directive has been encoded into you since your conception, and it revolves around a story that was central to our genetic religion, the original "fairy tale" I touched on in Part Four. The god Osiris was murdered and cast into The Nile, and his wife, the goddess Isis, went to rescue him. When Isis eventually recovered the body of her husband, she conceived a child by him, Horus, who eventually became king. Because Isis's husband was dead at the time of their reunion and conception of Horus, this was an *Immaculate Conception*, and all Egyptian kings were named Horus and seen as living gods born by Immaculate Conception. Hence perceived as a Virgin Mother, Isis was the most loved and popular goddess in ancient Egypt for her compassion and devotion to her child and to all the people. Isis can be identified with the FG-1 (Nurturer) Genetype.

After Caesar left Egypt, Queen Cleopatra gave birth to what is assumed to be his son, Caesarion, and Cleopatra seized the opportunity to create an image of herself as Isis, a "virgin queen," to foster stability in the region. Around 1,500 years later, Elizabeth I of England used the same tactic to unite a country that was tearing itself apart over religious interpretation, calling herself "The Virgin Queen" and someone who was "married to England." This Isis symbolism resonated with our ancient DNA that engendered harmony at both those times in history.

Approximately halfway between the time of Cleopatra and Elizabeth I, just when it seemed the ashes of The Goddess were gone forever, a legend was born out of The Dark Ages that echoed Isis's story in an abstract form with King Arthur and his knights, on a quest to recover what once was but was subsequently lost, *to restore balance* and prosperity to the kingdom. Arthur's power was derived from a matriarchal authority called The Lady of The Lake, and The Arthur Legend is based on a simple premise: that Arthur shall return; he shall be reborn.

The prevalent Egyptian image of Horus sitting on the lap of Isis is the model for The Madonna and Child seen in churches. The Virgin Mary is the only woman mentioned in The Quran, referring to her *seventy* times and as the greatest of all women. Embedded in our DNA is one master belief system with one core message, a genetic religion encoded by metaphor, and it honors *all* religions and spirituality today. Like an island chain in an ocean, we appear separate at ground level, but from below a common form unites us.

Top left: *Isis with Horus*

Top right: *Madonna with Child*

Left: *Persian "Maryam"*

The Virgin Birth is a metaphor for rebirth. Recovering your true self was an immaculate conception, *a birth that only requires one person to conceive.* This rebirth leads to "peace and joy" and an Authentic Life Experience. That is the *true* meaning of The Holy Grail. A Grail Quest is a quest to find The Divine in each of us, and now you have the map to do so.

You are here for a reason. Find what was lost, embrace your "spots," and pray with the words of William Blake: *Arise and drink your bliss, for all that lives is holy.*

Afterword: 2020s Vision

How will rapidly changing events affect you, and what can you do to best navigate through both the challenges and opportunities in the 2020s without sacrificing the ultimate goal of personal happiness? Many questions about many different matters will need *real-time* answering as the 2020s unfold, so this *You Code* afterword shall be a constantly updated one at:

www.JamesSheridan.com/2020sVision

More by James Sheridan

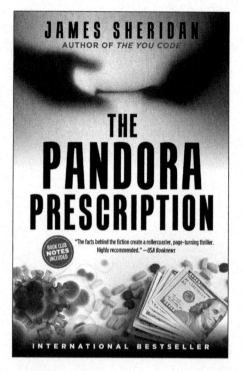

Author Dan Travis, a specialist on notorious unsolved mysteries, is on a book tour when a cryptic message plunges him into a silent war hinging on an incriminating data file. Finding it is Travis' only hope for surviving a deadly cross country chase. But to do so, he must discover the link between an extraordinary cover-up by Big Pharma and the assassination of JFK. The key lies within a secret underground of doctors sworn to an ancient oath. James Sheridan's crackling prose and driving narrative make this novel a white-knuckle ride through America's hidden corridors of power.

James Sheridan

James Sheridan is an international best-selling author, speaker, business consultant, award-winning copywriter, and founder of an Inc. 5000 corporation. Originally from London, England, Sheridan started from humble beginnings before embarking on an eclectic journey of diverse careers and accomplishments. He has been a professional ice hockey  player in Britain's premier league, the youngest regional sales manager for FIAT Auto Group, and a commercial airline pilot. His first pilot job included flying cargo to the Caribbean and secretive diplomatic mail flights from Miami to Cuba in unmarked aircraft as a foreign national. Later he flew 737s from London Heathrow.

Sheridan resigned his career as an airline pilot at age twenty-nine to start businesses, invest in real estate, and trade financial markets. He was determined to unlock the shortcuts and secrets of all aspects of life. He then passed on these shortcuts and secrets to tens of thousands of students around the globe through his highly successful company.

In 2007, after crossing swords with the medical establishment over a natural cure supplement, and determined to expose a medical cover-up, Sheridan wrote the fact-based novel *The Pandora Prescription*, which became a best seller in America and China.

Sheridan has dedicated the last twenty years to finding the definitive answers for humanity's biggest questions, and his new groundbreaking book *The You Code* represents the conclusion of his quest.

Connect with James online at:

 JamesSheridan.com

@FlySheridan